CW01543560

The MATCHMAKER
At your service

Dr Ezekiel Olusegun Alawale

FOREWORD by:
Pastor Matthew Ashimolowo

authorHOUSE®

AuthorHouse™ UK Ltd.
1663 Liberty Drive
Bloomington, IN 47403 USA
www.authorhouse.co.uk
Phone: 0800.197.4150

© *2014 Dr Ezekiel Olusegun Alawale. All rights reserved.*

No part of this book may be reproduced, stored in a retrieval system, or transmitted by any means without the written permission of the author.

Scripture quotations are taken from the King James Version (KJV) of the Bible—Public Domain.
Scripture quotations are taken from the Holy Bible, New Living Translation (NLT), copyright © 1996, 2004, 2007. Used by permission of Tyndale House Publishers, Inc., Carol Stream, Illinois 60188. All rights reserved.
Scripture taken from the Contemporary English Version® (CEV)
Copyright © 1995 American Bible Society. All rights reserved

Scripture taken from the The Message Bible (Msg)
Copyright 2002 Eugene H. Peterson

Scripture taken from the Good News Bible (GNB/GNT)
Copyright American Bible Society 1966, 1971, 1976, 1979.

Published by AuthorHouse 03/21/2014

ISBN: 978-1-4918-9889-5 (sc)
ISBN: 978-1-4918-9890-1 (hc)
ISBN: 978-1-4918-9888-8 (e)

Library of Congress Control Number: 2014904912

Any people depicted in stock imagery provided by Thinkstock are models, and such images are being used for illustrative purposes only. Certain stock imagery © Thinkstock.

This book is printed on acid-free paper.

Because of the dynamic nature of the Internet, any web addresses or links contained in this book may have changed since publication and may no longer be valid. The views expressed in this work are solely those of the author and do not necessarily reflect the views of the publisher, and the publisher hereby disclaims any responsibility for them.

Contents

Dedication vii
Acknowledgements.. ix
Foreword xi
Endorsements xiii
Introduction xvii
I Don't Want To Be Single 1
To Date Or Not To Date!... 10
Dating: Where Does God Fit In? 22
The Importance Of Knowing God's Will 38
Knowing The Will Of God 46
Courtship From A Christian Perspective 66
Watch Out For Red Flags In A Relationship 84
Preparing For Your Wedding.. 93

DEDICATION

I dedicate this book to God Almighty, my one and only true source of hope; my Saviour and friend. To my beautiful darling wife, Funmi; perfectly crafted and presented to me by The Matchmaker Himself, and to our dear children; Tosin, Toyin and Tomi. Thank you for your love, support and encouragement. I pray this book will spur you towards God's very best – His perfect will for your lives.

Acknowledgements

It is a common saying; success has many fathers. I would like to appreciate Pastor E. A. Adeboye, the general overseer of The Redeemed Christian Church Of God (RCCG), for the fatherly role he has played over my life and the ministry over the years.

This book will not have been possible without the persistent encouragement of one of my associate pastors, Dr Joseph Owusu-Nipah. Thank you for your support, help, loyalty and encouragement. You went through the manuscript times without number. May The Lord reward you abundantly. I appreciate you.

To my two 'partners in progress', Esther Opiyo and Angela Chrystal Kahendeke, most times, the long hours we spent on the book did not feel so long because of your delightful company. You both made the final work what it is. Thank you to Addico Japheth Ohatey for the animations you did single handedly.

To Rolake Akinsola and Pastor Simeon; your immense contribution made this book a reality. Your labour shall be rewarded. Thank you very much.

To my beloved Pastor Bode and Dr (Mrs) Kemi Akindele, thank you both for your genuine love for me and the work God has committed into our hands. Your advice and contributions towards this book are appreciated. Professor Gbolagunte Ojewola, Mrs Bukola Salako, Pastor

Tony Udeni, Pastor Jerome Obode and Mrs Yvonne Dawkins for offering useful advice as you went through the manuscript. Thank you.

It is the dedication of the great vessels God has placed in my life that has made this work seem easy. I would like to thank the Pastors of God's Vineyard Ministries; for their invaluable input to what I pray will be an enriching manual for the youth and singles of all generations.

Jesus' Hands and feet, the wonderful Staff of God's Vineyard Church, may God continue to strengthen you. To the entire membership of God's Vineyard Ministries and all who have contributed in their own special way, I appreciate you. I pray your lives will be saturated with God's abundant blessings as you serve Him.

I appreciate brother Gbile Akanni, you are a father over us. Your years of prayer, investment of time in counselling and guidance; first to my wife, and later to us as a family is very much appreciated. You are the man of God, the mentor, the big cousin that God used for Funmi not to miss Segun. You provided a shoulder for her to lean on. We are eternally grateful to you and sister Shade.

To my darling wife, Oluwafunmilayo Oyeronke Alawale. Without you, my life would not have been the same. You have been a source of strength and encouragement to me. You are truly a suitable help; designed for me. I appreciate you. To my children; Tosin, Toyin and Tomi Alawale, you have been wonderful children. Thank you for not only allowing, but also supporting me in doing what God has spared my life for. You are blessed.

To my God and Father: You brought me out of the horrible pit to a pedestal of glory, from darkness to your glorious light. You kept me alive. I cannot fathom why you so love me; there is no other God like you.

Foreword

The subject of relationships always provokes interest, particularly in this modern day; where access to the choice of a partner is 'made easy' at the click of a mouse.

This book gives a comprehensive approach to this subject; from dating, through courtship to eventual marriage.

Dr Alawale has certainly clarified a thorny subject from a Christian, Biblical and ethical perspective.

Marriage is made or destroyed by the values, vision and volume of truth the partners bring to the table. Love is not enough. Neither is emotion the foundation to build the edifice of marriage on.

The author gives us the signals of the spirit by which we may know if it is a YES, NO or WAIT.

Those who seek to know the truth will find the book quite enriching, enlightening and edifying.

Pastor Matthew Ashimolowo
Senior Pastor Kingsway International Christian Centre (KICC), London

Endorsements

'18 There be three things which are too wonderful for me, yea, four which I know not: 19 The way of an eagle in the air; the way of a serpent upon a rock; the way of a ship in the midst of the sea; and the way of a man with a maid.' (Proverbs 30:18-19 KJV)

Marriage is one of the richest and most powerful relationships on planet earth. It is a mystery that many find difficult to unravel. (Ephesians 5:32)

God ordained marriage for destiny and pleasure. It is an institution that allows you to let down your guards, expose your inner self without fear of destructive criticism and be without mask. It allows vulnerability without fear of betrayal. It promotes wholeness; breeds multiplication and can bring willing partners to the zenith of their aspiration, if practiced within the confines of God's knowledge.

Beautiful as the marriage relationship is, it can produce thorns when not initiated correctly. Many singles make wrong choices in the area of marriage because of ignorance and carelessness. People always say that love is blind, I agree but I add that marriage is the eye opener! So it's better to close one eye in prayer when planning to choose a life partner and open the other one in watching. Better stay single for life than marry the wrong person!

King David was a man loved by God. He sought God's leading in every battle he fought. But David was a failure in the area of marriage and family life, obviously, because The Bible never recorded one instance when he sought for God's guidance in his choice of a marriage partner!

> **5** *Trust in the LORD with all thine heart; and lean not unto thine own understanding.* **6** *In all thy ways acknowledge him, and he shall direct thy paths.* **7** *Be not wise in thine own eyes: fear the LORD, and depart from evil. (Proverbs 3:5-7)*

David's first wife was gotten by bloodshed, another by chance, another by availability and circumstance and another by lust of the eye and bloodshed. (1 Samuel 18, 25, 2 Samuel 11) Abraham, on the other hand, got a wife for Isaac his son by God' help. (Genesis 24)

Dr. Alawale's Book is a holistic marriage manual which covers extensively critical issues faced by singles.

In this book, he graciously dissects the Dating Myth and balances it with Biblical perspective; which will help singles make the right decision. He makes knowing God's will simple by sharing practical and first-hand experiences.

I trust The Lord to give this timely book great wings, like the eagle, so that it can soar to the Nations of the Earth and bless God's precious people; bringing great honour and glory to the King of the Universe, Jesus Christ the Lord.

Reverend Mrs Funke Felix-Adejumo
President and founder of 'The woman ministries', Nigeria

As I read through the manuscript of this book, I could hear the voice of a father and feel the compassion of the heart of a pastor. Written out of his wealth of personal and pastoral experience, Dr. Alawale has passionately presented God's view on dating and courtship that will answer many questions being asked today by young people on relationships and wedding preparation. This book is like a manual that will guide young men and women in laying a strong foundation for their homes and experience the very best relationship that God has designed for their lives. I recommend it to everyone, both young and old.

Pastor 'Bode Akindele
President, The Incubator International, St Paul, Alberta, Canada

Hats off to Dr Ezekiel Alawale for this masterpiece! His passion for young people and his many years of experience in helping shape destinies, pulsate through each sentence. I have no doubt that many will find good counsel and guidance in this book, and go on to build successful marriages.

Pastor Sam Adeyemi
Success Power International, Nigeria

Young people, wow, what a gift you are holding in your hands! Reading through this book, I can't stop thinking of how lucky you are. You live in a world of lies and deceptions. How precious it is, therefore, to meet somebody that tells you the truth. Truth, in a world of false, is in fact becoming a scarcity. This is why this book is so precious.

I, therefore, wish to express my deepest appreciation to Pastor Ezekiel; for taking the time from his very busy schedule to write this book.

Thank you and God bless you!

Pastor Sunday Adelaja
Founder and Senior Pastor of The Embassy of the Blessed Kingdom of God for All Nations, Ukraine

This is a book I recommend to all single people out there; both teenagers and mature singles. It is very insightful and deals with issues you are confronted with daily. It will also help in your understanding of dating; what it is and what it's not and how to enjoy the single life, as well as how to have a God centred relationship.

Dr. Ezekiel Alawale has been dealing with young people for decades now and the contents of this book are too deep to be missed! Parents, this book will be a great gift for your children and will also give you insight on how to guide them. Please get one for yourself, your friends and be blessed!

Pastor Owolabi Mebude
Youth Pastor of God's Vineyard Ministries, UK

The human brain doesn't come fully programmed at birth; it does not fully develop until our mid twenties. This means the pre-frontal cortex is not fully mature until then. This further implies that impulse control and judgement can be lacking.

Dr. Alawale has written a book that can serve as a bridge between the time of brain development to its full maturity, and the time of taking on the responsibility of marriage.

There is no fear of being politically or socially incorrect; the author simply, but courageously, states truths that can start any young person on a healthy course to a fulfilling married life.

Rev. Christie Bature Ogbeifun
Founder of Sine Qua Non Ministries, Port Harcourt, Nigeria

Introduction

We live in a world where popular trends, in many spheres of life, seem to evolve every passing day. Advances in science and technology in the last decade, for instance, have transformed the electronic media tremendously. These developments have introduced interesting dynamics into the modern trends of relationships. Internet dating websites, including Christian internet dating sites, are becoming increasingly popular. Some secular dating websites also give Christians the opportunity to connect with Christians only; if they wish to do so. Some sites even allow Christians to choose people from their preferred denomination. Some dating websites use personality tests to match people together while other sites even make it possible to establish compatibility before making decisions.

Beside such technological avenues, there are several modern ways people adopt, to initiate relationships. Professional matchmaking services are springing up everywhere; particularly in the Western world. Their job is to match people together for a fee. Another method is speed dating; which involves singles congregating in a room with only a few minutes to make a decision on a potential spouse. This is usually based on mutual interests and outward criteria.

Whereas some may find these channels helpful, I am quite sure many will agree with me that finding a successful relationship through these means will be purely based on chance. You will have to be really lucky to find your Mr or Mrs Right through these means. The question to the Christian reader is whether you would prefer to anchor your life on luck or on God's guidance. These ways are widely used by the people of the world, but many professing Christians equally resort to them in their search for their future marriage partner. The result is that the Church is experiencing about the same (if not higher) rate of divorce as others who do not believe in our God. Rather than risking one's destiny on imperfect human judgement, it pays for the believer to depend on God's unfailing guidance in such important matters as choosing life partners. Indeed, God is the only perfect matchmaker.

On the subject of depending on God's guidance in finding one's perfect spouse, or waiting for God's perfect will; there are several objections raised by some Christians. These include:

- 'God does not have a predestined spouse for any of His children'; some believe that as long as the person is a Christian and both agree to begin a relationship, God approves of it.
- 'There are relationships that had been purported to be of God, but parents did not approve of the person or did not agree to the relationship.' The question, then, is 'How can parents stop what God had ordained from the beginning?'
- 'What if those who are suited for each other live hundreds of miles apart; how would they ever find one another?'
- 'What if God gives me someone I do not love?'
- 'What if we are not compatible?'
- 'Why would God ask me to be in relationship with someone with whom I am not familiar?', and so on.

The answer to these questions is that God is perfect, loving and caring. He is sovereign and can do all things; we only have to trust in Him. He has promised not to give us a stone when we ask for bread or a snake when we ask Him for a fish. So you should not be afraid to know and accept His will when it comes to dating, courtship or marriage. He knows the best person for you. He knows your strengths and weaknesses as well as what you need to succeed in marriage and in life. He knows who is best placed to fill the gaps in your life. If you only dare to pray to, wait for and trust in Him; He will lead you to the right person.

As Christians, we know that God has a specific plan and future for everyone. We believe God is interested in each one of us and in every aspect of our lives. Furthermore, we believe that there is the perfect will of God in every area of our endeavours such as: Where we choose to live or work, what career we pursue, the location in which we establish and fulfil our ministry, and many others. In making these choices, children of God pray to God to lead and guide them. Why then, should such an important decision as the choice of a marriage partner, be an exemption? This book is intended to guide young men and women to experience the very best relationship that God has designed for their lives.

The Lord has blessed our Ministry with a vibrant and fast growing Youth Ministry. As I regularly minister to these young men and women who are genuinely hungry for the truth, I am usually confronted with many questions on relationships. This has laid a burden on my heart to write this book. As I relate with these young men and women who desire to fulfil God's purpose for their lives, I am motivated to ensure that none of them gets it wrong with their marriages. Marriage is a powerful institution; it can either enhance or destroy destinies. This book is born out of a burden to provide guidance for young people who are genuinely seeking to please God in all aspects of their lives. It offers an opportunity for young people to have the right foundation for their marriages.

This book has been designed to be a useful resource for youth groups in churches and fellowships. It will also offer help to parents who want to support and guide their young boys and girls to be prudent in handling issues on relationships. I trust that God will make it a blessing to you as you read through its pages.

CHAPTER ONE

I Don't Want To Be Single
SINGLE, YOUNG AND FREE

Being Single

We are all created with a legitimate need to belong. It is natural to want to feel accepted and loved. Relationships are an important part of our lives. As we mature into young adulthood, naturally, we have a drive towards more serious relationships. Almost everyone desires some form of a stable relationship. This legitimate desire can, however, be unduly heightened by the pressures of modern society. The standards and expectations of the society in which we live today put so much pressure on the youth; driving many into relationships without careful consideration of the implications. For many, this is where the challenges of relationships begin.

Singleness is often perceived as a phase to endure and not to enjoy. Many young people hate being single. Make no mistake about it; the fear of being and remaining single is real. The feeling of being left out, 'un-cool' or being the 'third wheel' is often dreaded; but should this be the case? I say NO! What we fail to realise as young people is that singleness is but a stage in our lives; essential and unavoidable. One should enjoy singleness and not just endure it. Many a time we are impatient and attempt to deal with the challenges of being single by rushing into relationships with high expectations that often turn to painful experiences. Desperation makes others ignore red flags or warning signs and enter into relationships blindly. So many young people have made bad choices as a result, and have experienced catastrophic consequences.

The pressure caused by loneliness is more serious in today's world. In Western countries like the United Kingdom, there are disintegrating family systems and social lives, which leave several people prone to loneliness. This has become a global phenomenon. People are left isolated as busy lifestyles and work schedules often fail to bridge the gap caused by the lack of true and vital close interpersonal relationships, such as those that you should enjoy in a family. Isolation is an unfortunate prominent feature of today's life. This is due, in part, to the growing culture of mistrust and selfishness. Isolation and loneliness coupled with mounting life pressures also account for rising incidences of anxiety, depression, substance misuse and violence.

Under these circumstances, loneliness is a genuine problem. However, one should not attempt to discuss or solve this problem by opening up one's life to just anyone; do not be indiscriminate. The truth is; you should not solve an immediate problem in a way that will create another one for your future. The right foundations must first be laid. The success of any relationship depends very much on having a right and broad perspective, as well as a mature and balanced concept of life. A well-informed decision should base not just on today's realities but also much more on long-term future considerations.

Aside from loneliness, another reason young people engage in relationships without careful consideration is a poor self-image. For example, in this state of mind, any young man asking a lady out can likely be interpreted as a sign of affirmation of her beauty. This person may, as a result, jump from one relationship to another or worse; end up being abused by the opposite sex. This is because, a person seeking affirmation in this way will be ready to go to any length to please the other person; just to keep the relationship going. Each time a relationship breaks and the other person moves on, they are left with a worsening sense of rejection and regret.

What Is the Essence of Singlehood?

Singlehood is a unique phase of life that you should maximise. The success of any future relationship very much depends on what we make of this period. Contrary to popular belief, you can enjoy life and have fun; fun that does not jeopardise the future! Singlehood is a time to work hard. It is also the time in which most of the life decisions you make can cumulatively affect what the rest of your life will be.

More than any other time, singlehood serves as a golden period to make life investment; you have the liberty to exclusively invest in and cater to yourself. No one would blame you. Singlehood gives you freedom to seize limitless opportunities and develop capacity in different aspects of your life; giving you a greater chance to succeed in life. It is a time to devote yourself to learning and make sure you develop as a person. Decision making is easier when you are the only one involved and do not have to fit your choices to another person's convenience or approval. You can exert yourself as you think fit to meet your personal developmental needs, desires and aspirations.

There is no better time to intentionally build your character than in singlehood. Good character or positive attitudes are essential ingredients in every facet of our lives. They find our highest altitude and enable us to keep and maintain opportunities that God presents to us. It is essential, therefore, to take full advantage of the resources available to you during this phase, to develop yourself for excellence.

> *Your best time to grow is in your single years*

Self development should not focus only on the physical dimension of your life. Man is a 'tripartite' being: a spirit with a soul that lives in a body. One should therefore aim to develop oneself holistically: Spirit, soul and body. Your core is your spirit. Everything living and healthy grows when necessary factors are available. As you grow up, the need for you to take responsibility for your growth and development increases. Nobody else needs to take this more seriously than you do. Biologically, balanced food and exercise are prerequisite conditions for our healthy growth. In the same way, spiritual growth does not happen automatically. The Bible says;

> *'I am the vine, you are the branches; he that abides in me, and I in him, the same brings forth much fruit: for without me you can do nothing'. John 15:5 NKJV*

Maintaining spiritual growth is all about connectivity. First and foremost, a branch that is not connected to the vine cannot access every ingredient necessary for its growth. In this light, we must keep up not only a constant, but also a close connection or relationship with God, our vine. It is The Vine that our spirit is dependent on; it is from The Vine that the spirit derives its nourishment. An intimate relationship with God is, undeniably, of vital importance to your spiritual growth and maturity as an individual. It will help you to develop or build a healthy character as well as godly values that will make you a jewel of inestimable worth.

Our relationship with God starts when we accept Jesus as our Lord and Saviour. Getting to know Jesus changes one's nature to a new nature; a godly nature. It makes one have a true perspective of life. It is then that you begin to discover how much God loves you. As you respond more to His love, you increasingly discover the true and pure love that no one else could show or give to you. You are then able to relate with Jesus as a dependable companion and a true friend. The vacuum in your life fills with joy and satisfaction.

A major avenue to therefore deal with the problem of emptiness in one's life is to build a relationship with God through Jesus Christ. He then becomes involved with you in your decision-making and gives you a new capacity for your life. No one genuinely cares for you as Jesus does. The taste of the pudding is in the eating! You can only know what a true, loving relationship is when you experience the model of true love. Your relationship with Jesus Christ will allow you to begin to understand what true love is.

Spiritual growth also results from reading, hearing, studying, meditating and living by the word of God. 1 Peter 2:2 NKJV says:

> *'As new born babes, desire the sincere milk of the word that you may grow thereby'.*

Spiritual growth also occurs as we relate with God-loving and God-seeking people. It is good to share in sweet fellowship with like-minded people around us.

Just as the right environment is essential for the growth of any living thing, the process of our overall spiritual growth thrives in positive environments and hampered in negative environments. In other words, there are environments which enable you to develop and keep up positive attitudes and values in life. There are also others, which will reinforce your weaknesses and urge you to express them. You must remember that whatever you feed grows; whether they are right or wrong attitudes, strengths or weaknesses!

It is important to bear in mind that people rise by their strengths and fall by their weaknesses. It is also true that while your strength may pass unrewarded, your weakness will attract penalty; good news doesn't make headlines. The friends you keep, the places you go and what you watch or listen to can decide whether you surround yourself with a positive or negative environment; these have tremendous power to influence your life.

Remember:
'Evil communication corrupts good manners' (1 Corinthians 15:33 KJV). The other part of your growth and self-development is in the nature of your mind. Note this statement from Scripture:

> *'Beloved, I pray that you may prosper in all things and be in health, just as your soul prospers'.* (3 John 1:2 NKJV)

Do you see how important having a healthy and prosperous mind is from this BIBLE passage? Your mind is a major part of your soul.

It is like a womb. If it is healthy, it will produce great ideas; if it is prosperous your whole life will be prosperous. Having a depressed mind depresses your whole being. Your mind determines the extent to which your body prospers. The fruitfulness of your life is dependent on how fruitful your mind is. You must therefore invest in your mind.

Your years as a single person are the best time for you to develop a healthy mind. As a young person, your single years are precious. You are young and free. You have opportunity, strength and freedom to discover and develop your mind to the best of your potential. During singlehood, you should therefore prepare yourself to balance your personality, both in character and in charisma.

> *The wellbeing of your mind is essential to your general wellbeing. Unstable emotions will destabilise and cripple your personality.*

You must take the initiative to develop yourself in skills acquisition, mental development and in what ever career you choose to pursue. Self development gives you the opportunity to rise to the top. Build yourself up for excellence instead of settling for mediocrity. Discover your potential; develop it and maximize your life. Remember: while it gets crowded at the bottom, there is plenty of room at the top! Aim for the top in your life; this is God's plan for you.

Celebrate Your Liberty

The time of your singleness is the time of self-discovery. You must constantly ask yourself, "WHO AM I?" It is essential to accept who you are, then do your best at being yourself; not someone else. In your bid to know yourself, you need to acknowledge your uniqueness. Each of us is uniquely packaged by God to best suit His purpose for our lives. That is why it is important to not only accept yourself, but also love and appreciate who you are in Christ. This will make you a happy, radiant person. You will find that it is only in placing true value on yourself in this way that you can carry yourself with dignity. No one can value you better than you. Remember you can only be your best when you are yourself! The value you place on yourself determines the value people will place on you. This reminds me of the story of the Israelites in the Scriptures, whose feeling of inferiority made them believe that other people saw them in the same light. In all honesty I would not be surprised if they did.

> *"We felt as small as grasshoppers, and that is how we must have looked to them."* (Numbers 13:33 GNT)

The time of your singleness is the time of self-discovery

Be true to yourself; discover your weaknesses and work on them. Discover your strengths and protect them; find your potentials and develop them. I cannot overemphasise that the time of singleness is the best time to develop your capacity; in terms of career, character and general attitude.

Developing yourself requires being intentionally self-motivating and diligent. It requires you setting goals and working on yourself to meet them. It requires making sacrifices and disciplining yourself to train. You must want to learn what you need to know.

Everyone needs a mentor; we all need accountability. Therefore, have an accountable structure that will urge you to work hard in developing the necessary components to help you maintain balance. Take advantage of your opportunities. Learn lessons from other people's experiences as well as your own. Discover what "fast tracks" people's journey to success.

Keep in mind that this is the 'freest' phase of your life: celebrate your liberty! Liberty, however, is not a license to carelessness or living without boundaries. Singlehood is the time to lay solid foundations for a life of integrity. Conform yourself to the principles of The Word of God and not to the ever-changing values of the world. You should mix widely but safely.

Once, I read a story of Billy Graham in the early days of his ministry. He and his team decided to set firm boundaries to avoid being in compromising situations with the opposite sex. According to Billy Graham, "if you lose your money, you lose nothing, if you lose your health you lose something but if you lose your integrity you lose everything". He laid firm foundations from the start. This is an element that has prevented scandals and earned him a high level of integrity and respect throughout the period of his ministry

Always remember you have only one life to live. Avoid compromising situations so that it is not messed up!

Chapter Two

To Date or not to Date!
WE'RE JUST GOING OUT FOR A WHILE

Dating

Many modern-day young believers find the concept of dating confusing. I wish to illustrate this using Cherry and Elena. Some readers may relate with the situation Cherry found herself in; leading her to seek guidance from her pastor. Others, with Elena's confessions. During a counselling session, a confused Cherry expressed herself to the pastor:

> *"How can I be feeling like this? I thought we were just friends without any strings attached. However, I'm falling for him deeply and I don't even know what to do! Pastor, we meant to stay just friends. Jay and I had a normal friendship. We went to the library together, were in the same study groups and even attended the same fellowship. We were practically stuck in the each other's circles. Somewhere along the line, I noticed that we were developing feelings for each other and we grew closer. Our conversations were longer and a little deeper than what I would consider in an ordinary friendship. What I really mean is that we have dated for a while. When I realised that my feelings for him were getting deeper and my emotions were running wild, I decided to seek God's guidance. Is Jay really the will of God for me? Will we get married in the future? Unfortunately, I cannot seem to hear anything from God. Pastor, can I make my decision based on my feelings for him? Would I have been more certain of God's will for me if I had sought God's face before dating Jay? Please, help me. I am really confused!"*

Elena was a member of the executive committee for her youth fellowship and adjudged by many as a committed Christian. With the issue of dating, however, she had her own views until experience taught her otherwise. Elena confesses:

> *"I've come a long way as far as concerns dating. My disposition had always been that you needed to know someone well enough to spend the rest of your life with them. This could only be done by going out with the person.*

If you found out that you didn't like them or realised that you are not compatible with each other; you then moved on and tried someone else.

To be honest, I did not even agree with the notion that as a believer, I could only marry a Christian. With this disposition, I actually experimented with a number of guys. However, I realised that every time I dumped a guy or a guy I had dated broke up with me, I got so depressed. In that sorry state, I became more vulnerable to anyone who would express interest in me. In trying to get myself back, I quickly gave in to any guy that came along; Christian or not. It never worked for me; most of those relationships ended up with worsening outcomes. Furthermore, every time a relationship failed, it felt as if I had lost a part of me. Right now I feel like I have lost my self-confidence. At this point in my life, after all I have been through; I find it difficult to trust anyone. Though I know better now, I am hurting deeply. I wonder if I can ever be whole again."

The Confusion

Like the scenarios above, I am often asked by several young people, whether by God's standards, dating is acceptable or not. As I write this book, the questions keep coming in:

- "For how long should we date?"
- "I like him but I don't know if he likes me in return. What should I do?"
- "How can I date, as a Christian, and not get intimate?"
- "We chat a lot more than I do with other friends, does this mean we are dating?"
- "Should I keep seeing him while I am praying to hear God's stand on this relationship?"
- "Is it alright for a Christian to date an unbeliever?"

- "Is it OK for Christians to simply date without having any intentions of getting committed to each other?"
- "I have prayed to God with regards to this person but God doesn't seem to speak back . . . ."

The questions seem unending.

Most readers can certainly relate with some or most of the questions above. This shows the level of confusion and ignorance on the issue of dating, especially within Christian circles. Thankfully, you will find answers to some of these questions in this chapter and throughout the book.

One major source of the confusion surrounding dating is the different ways in which people define the concept. It is important for us to look more closely at the meaning of the term 'dating'.

Dating: General Perspective

Dating, in one perspective, is a form of 'courtship'. Two people agree and decide to spend time together, engaging in different social activities; either privately or publicly.

Usually, the aim is to assess each other's suitability as a partner in an intimate relationship or as a spouse. Dating is commonly called a trial period in which two people explore whether they are compatible enough to take the friendship further towards a more permanent relationship. The two usually appear together as friends in public; they may or may not have sex, depending on their moral or religious convictions.

Others may use the term dating to describe a stage in a person's life when he or she is actively pursuing romantic relationships with different people.

The concept of dating is a relatively recent phenomenon, which has mainly emerged in the last few centuries. The practices vary considerably in different cultures, and from country to country.

> Who, desiring a brand new car, would settle for a damaged one; even after repair?

Personally, my understanding of dating is simply an act of asking someone of the opposite sex out on several occasions, to familiarise yourself with the person. The aim is to get to know each other well. Before committing to a long-term relationship, any two serious-minded people would want to know whether or not they are compatible with each other. Dating is a period when the people involved would want to prove whether they can get on well together; whether or not the other person meets their standard of a good spouse.

Allow me to illustrate the realities of this phase of a relationship with another scenario:

The concept of dating is like someone who wants to buy a car, but is not sure of the make or type of car to go for. Toyota? Ford? Jaguar? To be certain of which one will best suit their needs, the person may go to different dealers to test-drive the various cars. The practicality, however, is that when you test-drive a car, it is only for a few hours. There are a number of reasons why the car dealer will not let you to test-drive the car for a month or even a week. If that length of time is given, the car would no longer be regarded as new; it would be classified as 'a second hand' car. Moreover, if you are given too long a time to test-drive, it is possible for people to think that the car already belongs to you! More seriously, the longer you hang on to the car, the higher your chances of damaging the car! Assuming any of the above situations come to pass, do you suppose, upon its return, the car will attract the same value among other prospective buyers?

Quite honestly, who, desiring a brand new car, would settle for a damaged one; even after repair?

We can relate the above scenario to two young people dating. In a sense, we can consider dating as a 'test-drive' of a relationship between two people of the opposite sex; who seem to have mutual interest in one another.

Some people date for months or even years, without any definite commitment. Then out of the blue, after the entire community and acquaintances have known them together, one person walks away from the other. If you have ever been on the receiving end of such a situation before, you clearly know how it feels for someone you have been together with for months or even years to walk away from you. It is even worse when within weeks or months, the other person is found in a relationship with someone else. The 'dating concept' actually looks great; until you have been a victim of it!

The concept of dating must, therefore, be engaged in with some ground rules. Make this period short and conditional. We will consider this in detail later.

There is the need for great care in handling this period to prevent spiritual, emotional and physical trauma to either party. This is more so because at this stage, there is no firm commitment or conviction yet, which could give assurances of a lifelong relationship.

When I wanted to buy my car, I took it for a test drive, but I was given a specific time limit to do so. This experience helped me to discover several things I liked about the car; which further strengthened my wish and decision to buy it eventually. I was, however, very careful in handling the car to avoid any damage that could have caused the car to lose its brand new status. Since there was no firm commitment to buy the car during test driving, there was a limit to what I could do with it and the time to keep it in my possession!

To avoid becoming an emotional wreck from a failed dating experience, you need to set up clear and firm boundaries before you decide to go into it. The starting point is to ask and answer some sincere questions like:

- Why do I want to date him or her? – Get the motive right from the onset!
- What do I aim to gain from this experience? – Have clear and correct goals!
- How will I handle this in a way that I will not displease or sin against my God? – Set boundaries according to His Statutes in The Bible!
- How will I handle this in a way that I will not hurt myself or the other person in the long run? – Again, set boundaries!
- Do I consider myself mature enough physically, spiritually and emotionally to handle the relationship in a healthy and safe way? – Do not compromise your godly virtues and standards by exposing yourself to temptations that could cause you to fail in keeping your set boundaries.
- Do I have a sense of divine guidance towards relating with the person; or am I only responding to my emotions? – Don't run ahead of God; if you do, you get to a point that forces you to run back, after exposing yourself to pain and regret that could have easily been avoided!

"He that hath no rule over his own spirit is like a city that is broken down, and without walls "(Proverbs 25: 28 KJV)

Dating: The Christian Perspective

Our marriage relationship defines the value of our future. The success or failure of the marriage you enter into affects your destiny in a way that is second to none. There is an important link between our marriages and our life's purpose. That is why laying solid foundations right from the onset is important. Some important first steps to consider before getting into a dating relationship should include:

Your level of maturity or readiness:
Firstly, encouraging dating among young people who are clearly not mature enough for a relationship is not advisable. It is important that you are reasonably convinced that you are ready for a relationship before considering dating. There are occasions where young people at the age of fourteen have asked whether they can start dating. The question is, to what end would a person as young as that consider dating someone of the opposite sex? This obviously increases the chances of exposing oneself to unnecessary pressures that one is not mature enough to handle. Furthermore, this will also create great distraction to an individual in the pursuit of his or her academics or career. From an early age, the best thing to do is to learn how to develop and keep healthy relationships with people of the opposite sex. Making friends with people of the opposite sex is different from dating. The next chapter deals with the issue of maturity in detail.

The need to begin with God:
On attaining a reasonable level of maturity and readiness, an important step a believer should not leave out is prayer. It is essential to begin with prayer for God's guidance; just like we seek God's guidance in every other aspect of our lives where we need to make a choice. In other words, for a Christian, dating must begin with God. You should only take steps to engage in a dating relationship with the person God is leading you to.

> *'Trust in the Lord with all your heart; do not depend on your own understanding. Seek his will in all you do, and he will show you which path to take.' (Proverbs 3:5, 6 NLT)*

> For the Christian, dating must begin with God

It would not work the other way round; a child of God should not adopt a trial and error approach to find a life partner. If God is truly your Father and you have built a relationship with Him, it is not difficult to turn to Him. He is able to guide you in making such an important choice in your life; one which will have definite repercussions on His purpose for your life.

God leads us in different ways. This is further discussed in a later chapter. It suffices, however, to accept at this stage that God will not lead you to someone you are not attracted to. Our God will not impose anyone on you; He will rather support you to discover the person who best suits you and your life's purpose.

> *'Who among you will give your children a stone when they ask for bread? Or give them a snake when they ask for fish? If you who are evil know how to give good gifts to your children, how much more will your heavenly Father give good things to those who ask him.' (Matthew 7:9-11 CEB)*

The need for patience and consultations:
While it is important that you stay prayerful and sensitive to the Spirit of God always, it becomes all the more important during such crucial times of decision-making to depend more on God! Many people may come to mind or seem attracted to you. A sustained interest may begin to develop for an individual. One virtue you will need is patience; you do not need to rush to make a move! I recommend that you to have

a mentor. This is a trusted and mature person in your life; one who will be helpful for soliciting godly counsel in moments like this. It is helpful to involve them in such major life changing decisions and be accountable to them. You should willingly submit to this person for guidance, support and instruction; if need be, correction and rebuke. A mentor should have oversight in some capacity over you; for example, your pastor or a spiritual leader. Generally, a mentor is someone who is spiritually mature and balanced; worthy of your trust and respect. The lack of godly counsel and counsellors have accounted for many costly mistakes in life. The Bible clearly states that;

> *'Where no counsel is, the people fall: but in the multitude of counsellors there is safety.'* (Proverbs 11:13-15 AKJV).

Once two people are ready to commit to each other, they can then take pragmatic steps towards dating.

Getting the purpose of dating right:
Once these foundations are laid, the period of dating should not extend unnecessarily. This period should only be long enough for the girl to get confirmation and reciprocate the guy's interest, and for both to agree to take the relationship further in courtship.

Indeed the need for prayer, as explained earlier, is a two-way traffic; both parties considering a relationship must pray individually to receive personal conviction of God's leading.

> *'For all who are led by the Spirit of God are children of God'* (Romans 8:14 NLT)

Once the girl has the message of the interest being expressed, she needs the space and liberty to also pray without feeling pressured. This will enable her to receive a personal conviction as well.

Drawing from the story of Cherry in the first paragraphs of this chapter, extended dating can lead to strong emotional attachments and make it difficult for the interested parties to know what God is saying. It is very important for both people to have the space to seek God's face for certainty. The fact that the other person claims to have received a 'green light' from God is not enough; you need to have your 'green light' as well. This requires a great deal of patience and discipline.

These first steps bring two Christians to a point where they are both certain and happy to move on into a closer relationship. They are essential in establishing the right foundations and need not be compromised. Any building that will be strong and durable must have a good foundation.

> 'If the foundations are destroyed, what can the righteous do?' (Psalms 11:3 NKJV)

Anyone who is serious about having a good marriage relationship must not follow the world's selfish system. The world adopts a trial and error approach because in most cases their final goal is to have fun or pleasure. The non-Christian has no such thing as boundaries; after all, to them the greatest reason for a relationship is sex. Marriage is hardly the primary goal of such trial and error relationships. Even when it is, the world's concept of marriage has changed considerably in modern society. The world's standard on marriage is inconsistent with what The Lord wishes for His children. Christian marriage is a lifelong commitment; for better or for worse. Children of God must take advantage of their relationship with God—the benefit of having access to divine guidance. So we have no excuse to grobe around in darkness.

Lack of trust also causes many non-Christians to engage in multiple relationships; they do not know which one will work. As Christians, we being trustworthy and sincere is key.

As Christians, the basis of dating is to receive a clear confirmation that the person we intend to live with for the rest of our lives is truly the right person. That is why we should not compromise the foundations. Some of the issues I have discussed in this chapter are in detail, in the next chapter.

Chapter Three

Dating: Where does God fit in?
GOD BEFORE DATING

God's place in dating

Does God have a standard for dating? The Bible does not discuss dating explicitly, so how do I know God's place in dating? Is God in any way interested in being given a place in my dating process? If you have ever asked some of these questions, you are not alone. Yes, The Bible does not give a set pathway on dating. Pathways may differ depending on culture, personalities and several other factors. As a matter of fact, though we as Christians share the nature of God; we have different personalities, with different destinies set out for us individually. God is far too creative to have only one way to dating. What is certain, however, is that he has given us principles in His word to guide us in the process.

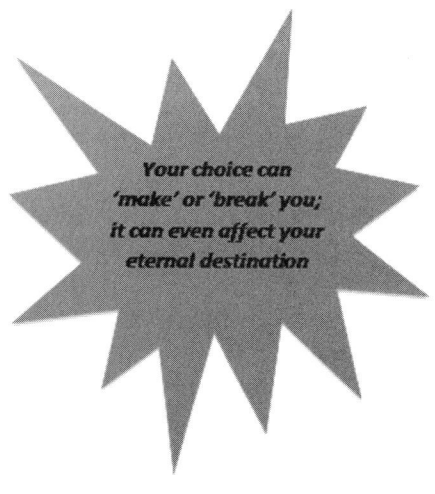

Your choice can 'make' or 'break' you; it can even affect your eternal destination

Remember there is no rehearsal with marriage. It is one of the most important decisions you will ever make in your lifetime. It's a decision that can either 'make' or 'break' you for life. The process leading to such an important state in your life is not one to take frivolously. Getting married to a person who is not best suited for you could ruin one's destiny. In fact, the decision could even affect one's eternal destination. From God's perspective, marriage is so important that He designed it as a permanent and unbreakable relationship *(Genesis 2:24; Matthew 19:5)*. This should give every believer the assurance that, if you give God the chance and involve Him in the process of identifying your best life mate, He will do everything possible to help you not to miss it. With dating being an important first step into marriage, God must definitely have a place.

This chapter provides a helpful pattern to follow to avoid common mistakes that many young people make in modern-day relationships; with long-lasting harmful consequences. These should by no means be considered as the formula or steps to perfect relationships. They are simply guides that show the principles in the word of God that could help you to set up your marriage relationship on an enduring and solid foundation.

Godly Dating: Taking the First Steps into Dating with God, Not just on your own

As a Christian, the need for you to first hear from God before stepping out to date anyone cannot be overemphasised. The dangers of jumping into a relationship on superficial grounds are so real in our world today; they clearly prove the sacrifice it requires in waiting on God for His guidance. Starting to date someone before taking steps to involve God could make it difficult to hear what God is saying about the relationship. Complications, usually orchestrated by human emotions, could shroud one's hearing. We are all emotional beings.

Becoming very close with anyone of the opposite sex could naturally lead to development of an emotional attachment by either one or both of you. Remember the law of magnetism; opposites attract! Mind you, emotions are strong!! They can overpower your spiritual antenna's sensitivity. In that state of mind, when God tells you that you are with the wrong person, you will not hear Him. Some may even attribute any warning signs from God as the devil speaking to them not to date or marry the person.

Emotions and feelings of 'love' often becloud our sensitivity to God's leading and guidance. In an atmosphere where emotional involvement fuels the ongoing attraction, you may not hear when God yells at you to run for your dear life. For most people, once their mind settles on something, it is generally difficult to acknowledge any warning or danger signs; even when they stare them in the face!

The emphasis is to never allow your emotions to go ahead of God. It will only increase your chances of getting it wrong. It is like putting the cart before the horse! It will be in your best interest to allow yourself be in a disposition where God's intervention is clearly perceived in matters of being in a relationship with the opposite sex; whether it is dating, courtship, or marriage. God, your Father, not only cares for you but also has plans for your marital life. If you trust in Him enough, you will seek His guidance in any major decision you make in life; more so in such a crucial one as marriage. The question is: Can you really trust God enough as your Father, to lead and guide you in the right way? This Scripture advises:

> *'Trust in the LORD with all your heart. Never rely on what you think you know. Remember the LORD in everything you do, and he will show you the right way. Never let yourself think that you are wiser than you are'* (Proverbs 3:5-7 GNB).

Sincerely, I will recommend that instead of depending on your shallow, limited and unreliable human wisdom; take advantage of having the all-wise and all-knowing God as your Father. Draw insight, knowledge, instruction, guidance and revelation from Him. Sadly, stories of heartbreak and failed relationships abound in the church today. Frankly speaking, many of these experiences happen because such Christians depended on their wisdom in place of relying more on God's ability to guide them in the choice of whom to relate with.

Dating before knowing God's mind often leads to heartbreak in both guys and girls; but less so with guys, as they are able, or tend, to easily move on into another relationship. Remember that in many cultures, it is men who go after women; hardly the other way round. It is very easy for a guy who has suffered a failed relationship to approach another lady he has interest in and let her know that he is available. On the contrary, not many ladies are able to leave such failures in the past and move on. Even when they do, in situations where the relationship was known to their circle of friends, it could take some time for others to become aware that the lady is available. Think about it; how many ladies will find it comfortable to go around informing others that their relationship has ended, and that if anyone has any interest in them, they are now available? In short, a failed relationship for a lady is not as simple as you might want to believe; it could mean several more years of lost opportunities and emotional pain.

Sadly, a common situation is where two people, who have been together in a relationship for many years, break up. Soon after, the man moves on, gets married, and unfortunately the lady remains single. I have observed relationships breaking up quite close to the wedding day and even on the day of the wedding. Can you imagine the trauma such a situation could expose one to? Situations like this leave the victim with bitter a disposition that could repel other suitors; one of whom could have been their best suitor. What a complete waste of opportunity!

God is the best match maker because He knows each one of us inside out (Psalm 139). He is the one who made, designed and packaged you. So, He knows the person who will best fit your life, calling, destiny, and personality. Above all, God knows who can help you to meet the life goals and purposes He has set up for you. Ensuring that you involve God guarantees that you will receive nothing less than the best.

Pitfalls of dating

As there are risks to test driving a car for too long, there are also some pitfalls in dating; especially when handled with immaturity or in an unhealthy and unsafe way. Some of the dangers in handling dating with frivolity include the following:

- **Emotional trauma**

As explained earlier, a usual result of disappointed expectations in dating relationships is deep emotional trauma and heartache for the one ditched. Such a person could find it difficult to trust anyone else. Some come out of the relationship as emotional wrecks, and may take a long time to recover from the agony. Some stay perpetually bitter, and may even go out on a revenge agenda.

One of my associate pastors told me an unbelievable story. A few years ago, a lady confessed over national radio, what her bitter disposition from a failed dating experience caused her to do to other men. She had dated a young man, who ditched her and vanished from her life after a short period of sexual escapades. She later learned, to her utter shock, that the young man was HIV positive and he was very much aware of it. Her blood tested positive for HIV and her anger drove her to sleep with as many men as she could, knowing that the virus would spread. According to her, all men were the same and they deserved double of what one man had done to her.

That morning, everyone glued to their radio as she persistently requested for the host to let her mention the names of people she had slept with. These included government ministers, some so-called

"Men of God" and people in responsible positions. She confessed that she specifically targeted high-ranking people, some of whom took her on their journeys to international conferences. The host at some point declared, '*listeners, the lady sitting before me in the studio is such a beautiful young lady; only a few men can resist her advances. I believe her story completely. The only challenge for me is that I cannot allow her to mention any of the names she has listed on the sheet she has handed to me; but I can tell you it has names of very prominent people we all know in this nation.*'

She said that she had come to that point of owning up after a true Man of God, to whom she intended to extend her ravaging advances, showed her what the love of God really means. Her evil agenda was only overpowered by the purity and the fatherly love of a single pastor. This, obviously, is an extreme case of how bitterness from a failed relationship could drive an individual; but it is a true life story.

- **Missed Opportunities**

The second common pitfall associated with dating in modern society is that many young people approach it as a trial and error experience, which lacks commitment. This concept makes some young people believe that they need to start dating as early as possible to try several relationships to gain enough experience by the time they are ready for marriage.

The danger of this frivolous approach to dating is that, while the dating lasts, it is possible to miss out on the real person God intends for you. Potential suitors may assume that you are already in a relationship. Many have missed their God-ordained partners in this way; having to settle for their second best. In effect, frivolous dating can cause you to miss God-ordained opportunities.

- **An Easy Platform For Pretences**

If your goal for dating someone is to get to know the person genuinely, brace yourself for serious disappointment! Dating, by its nature, creates an atmosphere for pretences. Whether you are a young man or a young lady, anyone who is desperate to keep up a relationship with you can do anything to appear nice and supportive.

Desperation has often led people to do the unimaginable. The only person who knows the true nature of a man's heart is God because He searches the hearts of men. He is the Only One from whom none can hide. We have all put on a fake front at one time or another.

Indeed, dating can present a platform for deception. Many receive the shock of their lives when they come to terms with the true nature of the person they have dealt with. Many have fallen into this trap and many more live with the regret for a lifetime. The only way out is to involve God from the beginning; He can show you the true colours of anyone you have interest in.

- **Temptations Towards Sexual Immorality**

In many instances, dating eventually becomes a platform for sexual immorality; people fail to set clear boundaries to guide them in the relationship. Spending time alone with someone of the opposite sex, whom you find attractive, can present temptations that are very hard to resist. It is imperative for Christians who intend to begin a dating relationship, to put boundaries in place from the onset and commit to respect them. If they find it difficult to keep the standards, they must seek counsel; otherwise with time, things can go horribly wrong.

- **Unwarranted Comparison**

Dating many people, as practiced among many young people today; including Christians, could present an unhealthy basis for comparison. Such practice can leave a person prone to comparing the person they eventually settle down with to the various people they dated in the past. This is more dangerous where the relationship involved sexual intimacy.

Many marriages suffer from such unwarranted comparisons, which on many occasions leave devastating repercussions on the sexual life of the couple. It has often led to cases of marital unfaithfulness, and in some cases divorce. It is an undeniable fact that several people contracted strange covenants, curses, diseases and illnesses by engaging in indiscriminate sexual encounters with different people they dated.

- **Loss of trust**

With every disappointment you experience, a worsening attitude of mistrust develops. As a result of the actions of those who have betrayed your trust in the past, it becomes more and more difficult to trust the next person who approaches you.

You may find yourself unable to commit to any later relationships; approaching them with an attitude of 'let's just wait and see'. This may further threaten the new relationship, resulting in another break up. In such situations, any later partner will suffer unnecessarily from lack of trust; causing frustration.

- **Loss of self-confidence and fear**

When a long running dating experience breaks up against one's wishes, it could easily lead to loss of self-confidence or poor self-image. This may progress into withdrawal, isolation and depression. You may also live with the fear that no one really wants you, and may end up seeing yourself as a 'bad person'. Usually, there is the fear that new relationships may not last; so in effect, you are jittery and nervous. On the other hand, fear could make you so desperate to hang on to the next dates at any cost; even if you have to compromise your values.

Making your approach

- **Advice for guys**

As explained earlier, it is only after you have known for sure that this is God's will for you, that you can then make your move towards dating a girl. You may do this by giving the girl hints of your interest. Even after being sure of where God is leading you, asking the girl out in an inappropriate way could stall the process and cause unnecessary delay or even denial. For example, some ladies in our Ministries' youth group, Radical Youth, have shared their different experiences with me. Let me list a few of the ways in which some guys have approached these ladies:

- 'I saw in my dream someone telling me you are my wife'
- 'I want to marry you'
- 'You are my wife'
  And so on.

It is very possible to get a negative response simply by the way you make your intentions known to someone you have an interest in.

- **Advice for ladies**

As a lady, once a guy asks you out several times, be sensitive and try to find out what he is really up to. Through effective communication, you could have a clear idea of his intentions.

Once the person's interest in you has been unmistakably confirmed, as explained earlier, you should take pragmatic steps to avoid emotional attachment as you seek God's face to receive your own conviction.

There are situations where a lady receives a conviction about a gentleman first. A lady in a situation like this could do one of the following:

1. Keep on praying for God to speak to the guy; leaving Him to work it out.

2. Confide in her mentor or pastor; who should pray along with her. It may, however, not be proper for the pastor or mentor to approach the guy on her behalf. Also, she must take care not to involve friends, who can easily slip the information and cause embarrassment.

3. Simply pray and believe God to create opportunities that will bring the two together.

4. Take pragmatic steps to make herself visible to the guy within boundaries. Establish a link; but not get too close, so as not to look desperate.

Whatever the situation, I would not recommend a lady to go ahead and propose to a guy. The man should hunt and chase after her. This will help to uphold her self-esteem as a lady.

> **Whosoever findeth a wife, findeth a good thing (Proverbs 18:22)**

Final admonishing on dating

As I close on the subject of dating, I wish to reiterate that the goal of dating is towards marriage; it is a part of the journey to finding a life partner. Although the word 'dating' is not found in The Bible, the ideas shared on this subject are based on Biblical principles that will make sure firm foundations are laid for a stable marital relationship. These may differ from the popular views in modern-day society, or not be fashioned according to worldly views.

Consider the following concluding nuggets carefully:

- **Christian versus non-Christian views**

The world's view on dating cannot be used as a standard for the Christian. God's ways contradict the ways of the world, and it is a failure for a Christian to pattern his or her life after the standards of this world.

The Scripture says

> *'If people have escaped from the corrupting forces of the world through their knowledge of our Lord and Saviour Jesus Christ, and then are again caught and conquered by them, such people are in worse condition at the end than they were at the beginning'* (2Peter 2:20 GNB).

The non-Christian may choose to date around as much as they want; this is not in line with God's pattern for His children. As a Christian, it is out-of-place to date around; sampling and testing your Christian brothers and sisters like the unbelievers do. The Litmus test: WHAT WOULD JESUS DO?

Another important issue that one should not overlook is to confirm whether the person expressing interest in you is a true believer in Christ. Many question whether a Christian can date or marry an unbeliever? The answer is a categorical NO! The Bible says two cannot walk together unless they are in agreement.

> *'Can two walk together, unless they are agreed?'* (Amos 3:3 NKJV)

For two people to live together successfully in a permanent relationship, they must have common orientation and shared values. There should not exist unequal yoking.

> *'Do not be unequally yoked with unbelievers'* (2Corinthians 6:14 ESV).

This is because you both have different philosophies of life and so your views on issues that affect your lives together will differ. Consequently both, or more commonly one, of you may have to compromise your core values to avoid constant conflicts. One person will constantly be subdued for peace to prevail in the home. What this implies to a Christian is the push to compromise your Christian convictions. Even your relationship and commitment to Christ becomes weak when you tie your life to an unbeliever in such an intimate way for the rest of your life. An unequally yoked relationship can cause you to miss out on God's purpose and call for your life.

Being married to a believer with a completely different background could also pose challenges. This however does not result in the same size of challenges as marrying an unbeliever. I believe God wants to spare us the pain and agony of being unequally yoked.

For these reasons, it is very important for you to find out if the person is truly born again as Jesus explains in John 3:3-8. He or she should share the same passion and desire toward Christ-likeness as admonished in Philippians 2:5.

> *'The attitude you should have is the one that Christ Jesus had'* (Philippians 2:5 GNB).

Many people seem to think that after marriage, they can convert their spouse. This is self deceit! You need to remember that nobody has the power to convert another person, only the Holy Spirit can.

Furthermore, be wary of pretences. Many people pretend they are someone they are not; be mindful, so you do not fall into the trap of deceit. Take steps to discover the character of the person before making any commitments. If the person has not been within your circle of friends, there are people in their life who can confirm their true identity, such as their Pastor, without necessarily making your intentions known to them. Be sincere and true to yourself.

- **Love and honour**

In a healthy relationship, the person you are dating should respect your values. You should never be threatened to compromise your standards to keep the relationship. Where there is true Christian love, righteousness is upheld. A person whose goal is to win your love and respect for the rest of your lives together would not want to take advantage of you, tempt you, or disregard your commitment to live a holy life as a true child of God. This is a key sign to watch out for in deciding to move the relationship to the next level or to end the idea.

Honour yourself, honour your date and honour God during dating

- **Age and Maturity**

Several people ask, how young is too young to start a relationship? It all depends on the individual's level of maturity, goals, self-discovery, and beliefs. Generally, the younger you are, the less mature you are; due to the lack of experience in life. As a young person who is just beginning to figure out who you are, you may lack enough firm ground; both spiritually and emotionally to set up a solid relationship. You are more likely to make unwise decisions that can leave you with emotional, physical, psychological, and spiritual damage. For instance, teenagers are often drowned by hormonal and societal pressures that may seem almost unbearable. They suffer from emotional instability which could dispose them to making unwise decisions on life changing issues such as relationships. You also need to remember that being in a relationship is more likely to expose you to temptations towards sexual immorality. Two immature people going through the transitions explained above are more prone to fall into sin.

The Acid test: If your consideration or readiness for marriage is still far off, it is probably too early to begin dating or courtship.

We can not pick a specific age at which we are synonymous with maturity. For instance, a 24-year-old boy may not match in maturity to a 20-year-old lady. Maturity is often seen in a person who has established life values; a mature person knows what he or she wants in life and where he or she is going. Such a person will be able to manage the challenges of a relationship better.

- **Set standards and keep them**

In dating, there should always be set boundaries; mutually respected by both parties. Make every effort to honour yourself, honour your date and honour God in your dating. As Christians, we have a calling to a higher standard of living; with The Word of God as our standard. We have the Holy Spirit to help us, so we must follow His promptings. We must take care of ourselves and be the best as God wants us to become His assets.

Take care not to tempt one another. It is wise to abstain from intimate forms of physical contact such as kissing, petting, necking or anything that would arouse your sexual passions. Sexual intimacy MUST be reserved for that glorious day of marriage; something to look forward to. You cannot afford to live a careless and carefree life. Avoid any atmosphere that could set a stage for sexual arousal. Making a commitment to abstain from every appearance of evil is the key that will protect you from falling into sexual traps that could cause destruction, regret and pain in later life.

Finally, let God be the beginning and foundation for your dating relationship and your marital life ahead. Having the right foundation in God gives stability upon which to build your future. If God is the author, you can guarantee His presence with you all the way. He will protect, sustain and prosper such a relationship.

> *If the foundations are destroyed, what can the righteous do?* **(Psalms 11:3 NKJV)**

CHAPTER FOUR

The Importance of Knowing God's Will

The Importance of Knowing God's Will

The Lord says, *"I will guide you along the best pathway for your life. I will advise you and watch over you. Do not be like a senseless horse or mule that needs a bit and bridle to keep it under control." (Psalms 32:8, 9 NLT)*

The passage above brings out some important points:

1. God says 'I will guide you'. God has offered to guide us in all our life decisions. We should take advantage of this for our own long-term benefit
2. There is the best pathway to our lives and God promises to guide us to it and walk us through it.
3. God says; 'I will advise you'. He will neither compel us nor impose His will on us. We are free to take His advice or ignore it.
4. It is clear that while we take to His advice, He will watch over us. We do not have that assurance if we go our own way and ignore His advice.
5. It is clear that if we reject God's leading in our lives, we will be acting senselessly and be forced to only learn from our own mistakes, in hard and painful ways!

Coming to terms with this scripture will give you the right mindset on the issue of divine guidance in every aspect of your life. It will hopefully make an impact on how you make important decisions about your life. Applying the principle of this knowledge to your life will save you needless and avoidable pain or regret from costly mistakes or error of judgement.

No matter where you want to go in life, you've got to head towards the right direction or you will never reach your destination. Would a person travelling from New York to London board any flight because it is a plane and it can fly? The fact is that though the person's wish is to go to London, it will be utterly disappointing for them to land in another destination! This error is due to assumption. Similarly, you could make costly errors by assuming that every Christian man or woman you admire, and would like to marry, could take you to your final destination in life.

Christian men or women may share some basic characteristics, but each one has a unique destiny or purpose in life. Every personal life has a design for a particular purpose, and so the person you are getting married to must have a similar life purpose to your own. It is then that both of you are the best companions; because your purposes are compatible and you are going to the same destination.

Only God knows what our life's design is for. In most cases, no one fully knows what his or her life was craftted for. Consequently, only God knows the best companion you should have to fulfil your destiny. Therefore, when it comes to relationships, it only makes sense to involve God who created you and designed your life for a specific purpose and knows the end of every one of us from the beginning.

There are several reasons why it is important to seek the help of God in choosing your life companion. These include the fact that:

1. There are choices to make among many ladies or guys. It is not all that glitters that is gold. It is not all that is good to you that is good for you!
2. There are uncertainties in life. When it comes to the important issue of marriage, which is a lifelong commitment; we need certainty with our choices. We cannot afford to gamble.
3. Seeking God's help will save you from the consequences of

basing your decision on assumptions, present credentials or only physical attributes. They are subject to change; things change and people change!

God has a definite Future for You
God knows your future ahead of time because He determines it. However, you will need to make the right choices along the way to lead you into the future He has for you.

> *For I know the plans I have for you,"* says the L*ORD*. *"They are plans for good and not for disaster, to give you a future and a hope.* Jeremiah 29:11 *(NLT).*

You don't know the way there: God does!
The truth is, no matter how precious and great God's plans and purposes for you are, you don't know how to get there except He Himself shows you the way. This is why it is risky to base the choice of a marriage partner only on physical characteristics. These are subject to change and they will change! Besides, physical characteristics are not all that build a home! Character is more important than charisma. In fact, God said:

> *Only I can tell you the future before it even happens (Isaiah 46:10 NLT).*

It is, however, your responsibility as a true child of God to seek to know God's perfect choice for you. This is a general principle which is applicable to every aspect of our lives. Consider God's word in Ephesians 5:17;

> *Wherefore be ye not fools, but understand what the will of the Lord is (ASV).*

With regards to the need to seek God's guidance in choosing a marriage partner, you may ask, *'Does God really know who I will marry? Does He actually have someone in mind for me? Can I not just marry anyone, especially if they're Christians? Is it only one person God has in store for me?'* and so on.

The answer to all these questions is that God has a perfect will for you in every area of your life; including your marriage partner.

> *'Do not conform any longer to the pattern of this world, but be transformed by the renewing of your mind. Then you will be able to test and approve what God's will is—his good, pleasing and perfect will.'* (Romans 12:2 NIV)

The truth is that God will not impose His will on you and me. He desires to lead or guide us to what is best for us. He desires to lead us based on the knowledge He has on the needs of our lives. It is all for our sake. God's guidance on many occasions has saved me from many actions which would have destroyed my life.

> *'Trust God from the bottom of your heart; don't try to figure out everything on your own. Listen for God's voice in everything you do, everywhere you go; he's the one who will keep you on track. Don't assume that you know it all. Run to God!'* (Proverbs 3:5-6MSG)

Moreover, as the all-seeing and all-knowing God, He alone sees and knows what you may never see or know about the person you're considering for marriage. For example, God knows the future of that person. He knows their capacity for the journey ahead and what they can do in the future; which they may not even know about themselves.

This reminds me of a story of one of my friends in the Medical School I attended; we attended the same fellowship. He was praying for God's guidance on the person he would have as a wife. Like it is with many of us, there were a number of beautiful, godly ladies in the fellowship whom he could consider. Each of these ladies was unique but different. They were different in ways such as their potentials and gifting, in their strengths and weaknesses, in their likes and dislikes, in their dreams and aspirations, and in their purposes and destinies.

During the course of his prayers, one night he had a dream. In the dream, he saw himself in a show room of a Peugeot assembly plant. All the cars were brand new but with different colours, and different models. My friend's favourite colour was blue; like me! So my friend, without any second thought, went straight towards a blue coloured car. As he approached the car, the plant sale manager came to him. He said to him, 'let me help you in making your choice. I know more about these cars than you do. I know the one whose performance will suit your long-term needs. The colour is the least important, it can fade, you can change the colour at any time and above all, the level of performance of a car does not depend on its colour!' My friend woke up from his sleep and shared this dream with me. The message was clear. He had learned his lesson; he was not going to let looks deceive him!

The success of your marriage influences the wellbeing of our society
The marriage relationship is the first human institution established by God and probably the most important. Among others, marriage purports to give companionship among spouses and offer the basis for a stable family life. Marriage is the bedrock of the society. A stable marriage produces stable and happy children; who are the hope of the future generations. There is a direct correlation between the breakdown of marriages and youth violence in our societies. There is also a direct relationship between healthy families and the health

of our society. Jesus taught us to pray *'your kingdom come, your will be done on earth as it is in heaven'. (Matthew 6:10 NIV)* In effect, the success of your marriage has a direct bearing on God's will being experienced on the earth; just as God desires.

It is important to involve God
If you allow God to author your marriage, you can be rest assured of His presence throughout the journey to defend it. Whenever there is any challenge in your marriage, you will be able to turn to God for His help or support. Besides, there will be peace and assurance which comes with knowing that God is in your marriage from the beginning. This will not only give you the confidence to ask God for his help and wisdom from time to time in your journey of life, but it will also help you to give your marriage all it takes to make it work; because you know you got it right from the beginning. During challenging periods in the journey of your marriage, you will not have any doubt whether or not you have made the right decision.

Indeed, the need to depend on God and trust Him for guidance, through the process of identifying and choosing the right person for your life, cannot be overemphasised. God has promised to guide you. It is your responsibility to make use of the wisdom and grace He has given you to discern the person He is leading you to. Although He knows who best fits your life, He will not force His will on you, but rather leave you to choose in line with His principles.

The key is to submit your will to the Lord's; it is important for you and me to have absolute trust in His ability to lead us correctly. We must know and be convinced that God loves us dearly; He leads us on the basis of His love for us and in the interest of our long-term good. Discerning God's will for your life about marriage is vital.

God is good! If you seek Him, you will find Him; He will lead you to your dream spouse!

In the next chapter, you will come to a better understanding of the role you have to play in making the right choice, as you carefully seek to follow God's guidance and leading.

CHAPTER FIVE

Knowing the Will of God
HOW DOES GOD LEAD?

Knowing the Will of God

'Dance with God, He'll let the right person cut in' (Unknown)

My Wife's Testimony of How we Came Together

At the tender age of 10, due to the experiences I had observed around me, I decided as a little girl to pray to God to give me a good husband. My heart's desire was to have a husband that would not beat me; but one that would love and care for me. I had seen the incessant abuse that our neighbour had experienced from her husband. He would not only fight with his wife but also throw the dinner plates out through the windows. I had never seen my parents argue or fight, so I made the issue of the right husband a prayer point every time I went before God in prayer. It was years after I became born again, that I realised how Christ Jesus could transform the life and home of the believer.

Just before I started my A level education, I met Brother Gbile Akanni, a Man of God. I did not know him at that time, but discovered he was in fact my big cousin. He told me God asked him to talk to me about marriage. I told him I was still young and that I still had a long way to go; as I intended to study medicine. He said God had instructed him to discuss this with me, so I agreed to talk with him. He told me about the need to pray and seek God's guidance about His will for me in marriage. He also told me that the last decision in the choice of whom to marry depends on the woman. He advised that when the time comes, I would need to make my decision based on my own convictions and testimony; and not on the man's testimony.

He also said I should take care when accepting gifts from any man who was seeking my hand in marriage; explaining that this gesture might influence my decision whilst seeking God's face. The counselling was thorough; it helped me tremendously and gave me a good basis for the choice I eventually made.

Just two weeks after our meeting, some Christian brothers approached me with 'big' testimonies; asking me to become their future wife. In some cases I thought to myself, 'Wow! That was a fantastic testimony; this surely could not be a wrong choice!' At that point, I remembered the counsel that I had received; 'big brothers' in Christ could make mistakes, and I needed to have my testimony. My decision to say yes to any man had to be based on what God was saying to me. The Man of God had explained that it was my testimony from God that I could lean on in times of challenges in the future.

During those times, The Holy Spirit gave me a word from Psalm 32:8 which says, *'I will teach you in the way you should go; I will guide you with my own eyes'*. Throughout this period, I held on to this word and kept seeking God's face. The man of God also continued to pray for, and counsel me while I gave him feedback on how things were unfolding.
During the vacation in my last year of A-level, I decided to wait on The Lord in 3 days of prayer and fasting. I locked myself up in my room and poured my heart out to God; I was tired of brothers coming to me and I needed him to sort me out. I asked God to lead the right man to me before the end of the week; reminding Him of The Word He had given me. On that Thursday, the man who became my husband approached me; asking to meet somewhere to discuss something important.

He was the only brother whose thoughts and feelings towards me I had no earlier inkling of; unlike others' proposals. He was tutoring a group of us from our fellowship in preparation for Physics A-Level examinations. When he asked for us to meet up, I just thought he wanted to discuss the teaching sessions; as I was the coordinator. To my greatest surprise, he proposed our courtship!

I asked him to wait as I prayed about it; he agreed. For some reason, from then on, I became very nasty towards him. Each time I behaved inappropriately, however, The Holy Spirit would prompt me to acknowledge my wrong; and I would ask The Holy Spirit for forgiveness. I maintained this disposition towards him for some time; I kept repeating the nasty behaviour over and over again. Surprisingly, I never behaved like this to any of the other brothers that had proposed till he showed up. By this time, The Holy Spirit had convinced me that he was the one for me, in two different ways.

However, I was a bit confused because there was a different brother in the Fellowship whom I thought was the will of God for me. There had been issues in that brother's life, which I considered as problematic. I had spared no effort in interceding for him, and God had answered. In all honesty, he was the person I was expecting to propose to me instead of my husband. So I asked God, 'What is happening? What about this other brother?' God then made me aware that He had put him there to distract me from considering all the other brothers that had come to propose to me earlier. The Lord then told me that the brother was already engaged, nearly married and gave me the name of the lady as well as the name of the city where she was living. This was later confirmed to me when my friend visited that city and delivered a message for him to that lady.

I met with my mentor, the Man of God, one evening and updated him on all that had happened; he suggested that I write letters to all the brothers awaiting my response. He said I should let them know my situation and ask them to pray again. We prayed in agreement that evening, asking God to show me the message in the letter from my future husband; to avoid any confusion.

Something amazing happened in the early hours of one morning: I woke up and saw a hand, writing on the wall of my room. I thought I was dreaming! I got up in fear and picked up my pen and diary to write the mystery outlined as points 'a', 'b', 'c', 'd' and 'e'. I wrote everything down to the last word and when I looked up, both the hand and the writing on the wall had disappeared. Afraid, trembling and crying, I prayed in the Holy Ghost. This woke my sister who asked what the problem was. I said, 'Nothing'. She asked, 'Then why have you been crying, and why are you so distressed?' I could not talk, so she started praying as well. Later that morning, I went to meet my mentor. He was so calm, as he said, 'but that was what we asked God for, were you not expecting Him to answer?' I admitted that I never expected anything close to the dramatic manner in which I saw the revelation. He said, 'God is faithful.' He then instructed me to keep this to myself while we waited on the brothers' responses, to make comparison with the writing on the wall.

I received various replies from all of them justifying themselves. One of them even wrote a wonderful 7 page testimony on how he knew I was his wife-to-be. My husband's letter, however, amazed me. His writing matched God's writing on the wall word for word; to the point of outlining each point as 'a', 'b', 'c', 'd', 'e'. Not in the order of '1', '2', '3', '4', '5', or even Roman numerals; a common method in writing at the time.

My mentor asked, 'What do you think?' I said, 'I now know that he is the one.'

I then arranged to meet with him to let him know of my decision; after an 8 month wait. In that time, he had patiently endured my hostility. Since then, every time he talks about the way I treated him, I feel so ashamed. I know the devil wanted him to get discouraged and go to another sister. If that had happened, not only would I have missed God's best, but he and the woman he could have married would have missed God's best too. God gave him enough grace to bear with me and wait. I thank God for that!

He was both surprised and happy at my request to visit him. He agreed. On the visit I told him of how God had confirmed to me that he was my husband-to-be. We prayed together and this was how our courtship began. We met with our fellowship president and informed him of our decision; he asked for our testimonies, separately, and then prayed with us.

Today, I have no regrets about my choice, it has been glorious! Even in times of challenges, there is the peace that I have always had; assuring me that God is in it. He has always been faithful. Glory to God for His love, goodness and faithfulness! He is a good God indeed. He knows the end from the beginning and if we give Him the chance, He will bring us to the good end.

> *Declaring the end from the beginning, and from ancient times the things that are not yet done, saying, My counsel shall stand, and I will do all my pleasure* (Isaiah 46:10 KJV).

This is how our story began. Day after day, we both remain grateful to God that we did not miss each other. God is no respecter of persons; He still does these things today. We must give Him the chance and trust Him to do it.

When Should I Start Praying?

There is no hard and fast rule as to when to start praying about whom to marry. However, it is best to begin early enough; long before the pressure mounts. Some people have Christian parents who regularly pray for them on all aspects of their lives; including their future homes which makes a lot of difference. However, this is not the case for everyone. You, therefore, need to take responsibility for your life as early as possible. As you pass the issues of your life to God in prayer, you allow Him to take responsibility for your success.

Whatever your situation, the first and most important key is to understand how God speaks to you. This is enhanced by the depth of your relationship with God; just as it is with our physical parents or close friends. Hearing from God then becomes your daily and growing experience; you should develop in it. There is also a direct correlation between the depth of our relationship with God and our sensitivity to the voice of the Holy Spirit.

Secondly, another key that will help you learn how God speaks to you is in the small day-to-day decisions and choices you make. This enables you to learn from your experiences; discerning whether God is directing you or if your mind is suggesting something. Your Spiritual perception is then sharpened and becomes more accurate as you reflect on and take stock of these decisions. The different outcomes help you to fine-tune and develop consistency in knowing how God speaks to you. In times of big decisions, therefore, there will be certainty that this is God leading you because you are familiar with the ways in which He deals with you.

It may not be spectacular, and it does not have to be spectacular to be supernatural and authentic! It may not make spiritual sense to others, but it will make sense to you because you know it! More importantly, whichever way God leads you, your decision must conform to His written Will.

> 'Look to God's instructions and teachings! People who contradict his word are completely in the dark.' (Isaiah 8:20 NLT)

The third important key is discovering and living for God's purpose for your life. As you connect to your purpose and live for the Kingdom, all other things that you need in your life; including your choice of spouse, add to you at the right time! I wish to reiterate that God has planned a great future for you; neither one of you can do it alone. You need to walk hand in hand with Him; in cooperation and interdependence. Pray, generally, for yourself so that you can discover God's will for your life and to live for it.

The wife or husband you will eventually marry is the greatest asset and companion you will have in your entire life. God desires to help you make the right decision.

> *He who finds a [true] wife finds a good thing and Obtains favour from the Lord.* (Proverbs 18:22 AMP)

Do not wait until you are emotionally attached to somebody before you begin to pray. Emotional attachment makes it difficult for anyone to know God's will. You will have to find the person yourself, all God will do is guide you. Do not wait until after your parents and friends start putting pressure on you before you begin to pray. This will make you desperate and impatient. Also, do not wait until you become too close with the opposite sex before you begin to pray to know whether they are the right person for you. It gives room for error and makes it more difficult to pick warning signals or red flags.

How does God lead?

> *The Lord is my shepherd, I shall not want . . . . He leads me . . . . (Psalm 23:1-2 KJV)*

- 'Does God want to lead us?'—Yes, He wants to!
- 'Does God still speak to man?'—Yes, He does!

- 'How then does God lead?'
- 'Should God have a say in what I want to do or the choice I want to make?'

These questions about God's will and leading are severally asked. If there is one thing God loves and enjoys doing, it is to lead and guide His children as they live and walk through planet earth as 'strangers and pilgrims'.

As God's dear son or daughter, He wants to protect you and prevent you from making costly mistakes in life by leading you. Therefore, in this chapter, we will look at the various ways in which God leads His people; not only in making decisions about whom to marry, but also about every aspect and issue of your life.

God leads His children. In fact The Bible says:

> '*for as many as are led by the Spirit of God, are the sons of God*' (Romans 8:14 KJV)

Why is it important for God to lead us?

Man has always required help to find the right way or direction to his destination; especially when he is in unfamiliar terrain. Before the era of development and technological advancement, people relied on others for directions. When you got to a cross-road, you asked for directions. Without this, there was chance of missing your way and never getting to your destination. Over the ages, as we have enjoyed the advances in development; we are more dependent on devices to find our direction. We have advanced from the use of 'The A to Z' Map Guide to the 'Global Positioning System' (GPS). Travellers on land, sea and in the air; including the military forces at war, use this device to find their locations and directions in unfamiliar terrain.

Similarly, in life, we need help with direction into the unknown. The underlying truth is that man does not know everything about the present, and is also uncertain about the future. Choice making is part and parcel of everyday life. For every good thing, there are options which may all seem good. God's interest is in leading us in every area of our lives, but we must seek Him and be ready to follow his instructions.

One of the reasons why we pray, as Christians, is for divine guidance; we seek His help because we know we have limits. Just as God led my wife in her quest to know who her husband would be, He gives us this assurance in His word: *'I will instruct thee and teach thee in the way which thou shall go: I will guide thee with mine eye'* (Psalm 32:8 KJV).

The Bible compares a man who does not live by God's leading to a horse, or a mule, *'which have no understanding; whose mouth must be held in with bit and bridle, lest they come near thee'* (Psalm 32:9 KJV). We must not live our lives in ignorance when God is ready to give illumination, knowledge, insight or foresight into the issues of our life that we do not fully understand.

How Then Does God Lead Us?

The following are some of the channels through which God leads His children in life. Depending on how God usually leads you, you could be guided through any of them when it comes to deciding on the person to spend the rest of your life with.

1. His Word

The primary and most important way by which God leads His children is through His Word—The Bible.

Let me share my story with you. I remember when I was going to choose who would be my wife during my second year of University. At the time, my extended family were experiencing a lot of demonic attack, so I gave God one condition; that I do not want someone who is not a genuine Christian. I told myself, 'I cannot afford to fight these same battles in my home, or with my own wife!' In fact, the various Christian teachings that were prevalent then did not help issues either; Christians would cast out devils in almost every situation.

As I continued praying and looking up to God; the name of the woman I am now married to dropped in my spirit, and this persisted. By this time, I had known her for about two years, as we were attending the same Christian fellowship. She was becoming more attractive to me, compared to the other ladies, in the same fellowship. My love for her was growing. I began to pay attention to her personality, her gentleness, and her demeanour; there was an aura of responsibility around her. She was simple and quiet and she loved God.

However, due to the situation my family was facing, despite the convictions I had received from God about her, I still insisted on being sure that she was not 'demon' possessed! It is true that the different circumstances of our lives and backgrounds can influence the conditions we present to God. Thank God, He understands us and takes our dispositions into account whilst leading us.

I maintained this disposition until one fateful day, as I studied my daily devotion, 'The Daily Bread'. I read from the book of Acts 10:1-16. It was an account about God asking Peter to go and preach to the first set of Gentiles; that was, Cornelius and his household. At that period of time, the Jews generally discriminated against the Gentiles. Peter would not ordinarily interact and preach to Gentiles because it was 'forbidden'. Let us read The Scripture account in Acts 10:9-16 NKJV, together.

> *⁹ The next day, as they went on their journey and drew near the city, Peter went up on the housetop to pray, about the sixth hour. ¹⁰ Then he became very hungry and wanted to eat; but while they made ready, he fell into a trance ¹¹ and saw heaven opened and an object like a great sheet bound at the four corners, descending to him and let down to the earth. ¹² In it were all kinds of four-footed animals of the earth, wild beasts, creeping things, and birds of the air. ¹³ And a voice came to him, "Rise, Peter; kill and eat."*
>
> *¹⁴ But Peter said, "Not so, Lord! For I have never eaten anything common or unclean."*
>
> *¹⁵ And a voice spoke to him again the second time, "What God has cleansed you must not call common." ¹⁶ This was done three times. And the object was taken up into heaven again.'*

Very specifically and strongly, the phrase 'What God has cleansed, you must not call common or unclean' jumped at me and stuck to my spirit. Led by the word of God, I proposed to her. And to this day, I have no regrets marrying my darling wife.

When people who knew us heard that we were going out, they wondered what our lives and home would be like. This is because we were both quiet and shy! However, if you know us, or even visit our home now, you will be able to judge who was wrong; the people or God. You can imagine how the physical characteristics we know about people are so subject to change over time. God knows the future; the changes that will take place in our lives and what we will become tomorrow. This is why it is all the more important to rely on Him for guidance.

Let us consider this Scripture together:

> *'To the law and to the testimony: if they speak not according to this word, it is because there is no light in them' (Isaiah 8:20).*

This implies that the gold standard of God's leading is His word; it is the standard by which you should judge all other methods. In order words, whichever way God leads you must agree with The Bible; The Word of God.

2. The Inner Witness

> *'The spirit itself beareth witness with our spirit, that we are the children of God'. (Romans 8:16, KJV)*

The spirit of God bears witness with our regenerated human spirit. This is a knowing deep down in you. It is an agreement in your spirit or a persistent impression on your mind. There is inner peace each time the thought comes up in you. There is inner joy welling up in you as you pray or think about it.

Interestingly, in the Old Testament, this is the way the high priest knew the mind of God. Any time the high priest was to judge the people while they come before him with their issues, he wore the breast-plate, and put the Urim and Thummim in the pocket of the breastplate; lying directly over his heart. The Urim represented light while Thummim represented truth. The Urim glowed and produced some heat which would be felt by the high priest on his chest wall, over the heart any time someone told the truth. This confirmed the mind of God to the high priest which he then upheld.

> *'And thou shalt put in the breast plate for the judgement of Urim and the Thummim and they shall be upon Aaron's heart, when he goeth before the Lord: and Aaron shall hear the judgement of the children of Israel upon his heart before the Lord continually'* (Exodus 28:30 KJV).

This happened then because the Holy Spirit was not residing permanently inside of anyone, including the high priest. This was a shadow of what was to come. Today however, The Holy Spirit has a ministry that is permanent in the life of a believer. Jesus said, *'. . . that he may abide with you forever, even the spirit of truth'* (John 14:16-17 KJV).

The Holy Spirit can give you a check in your spirit when you want to do something; to show you whether or not it is the will of God. This 'check' may come as sudden fear, loss of sleep or agitation in your spirit. These are warnings against the wrong decision.

Some people call this intuition or a sixth sense. When The Holy Spirit leads you, you are usually unable to explain why. You just know deep within you; 'this is it' or 'this is not it.'

The more you pay attention and acknowledge it, the more right or sharper you become in discerning the voice of the Spirit. The more consistent you are in submitting to The Holy Spirit, the more sensitive you become and the greater your confidence to work with it.

3. The Still Small Voice

> *'And thine ears shall hear a word behind thee, saying, this is the way, walk ye in it, when ye turn to the right hand and when you turn to the left'* (Isaiah 30:21 KJV)

God speaks to me a lot through a still small voice. Sometimes, when I am praying, an original idea just drops in my spirit. Many times, it is when I have finished praying and I'm just lying down, or I may even be in the shower; when the still small voice comes distinctly. Usually, the exact time such voice or idea comes is unpredictable. This is what makes it unique. More often than not, the idea lingers.

Allow me to share an experience to illustrate this reality. About two years ago, the Ministry hit a financial low; we were contemplating not hosting the annual Women's Conference. The leadership had agreed to suspend the event and the staff felt it was a reasonable decision. A few days later, while in the shower after my morning prayer; there was this still small voice that said to me; *"if you only consider what you have physically at hand before you do My Work, you will limit Me"*. It then flashed the story of Jesus feeding 5000 people with five loaves of bread and two fish in John 6:1-13.

> *"After this, Jesus crossed over to the far side of the Sea of Galilee, also known as the Sea of Tiberias. A huge crowd kept following him wherever he went, because they saw his miraculous signs as he healed the sick. Then Jesus climbed a hill and sat down with his disciples around him. (It was nearly time for the Jewish Passover celebration.) Jesus soon saw a huge crowd of people coming to look for him. Turning to Philip, he asked, "Where can we buy bread to feed all these people?" He was testing Philip, for he already knew what he was going to do. Philip replied, "Even if we worked for months, we wouldn't have enough money to feed them!" Then Andrew, Simon Peter's brother, spoke up. "There's a young boy here with five barley loaves and two fish. But what good is that with this huge crowd?" "Tell everyone to sit down," Jesus said. So they all sat down on the grassy slopes. (The men alone numbered about 5,000.) Then Jesus took the loaves, gave thanks to God, and distributed them*

> *to the people. Afterward he did the same with the fish. And they all ate as much as they wanted. After everyone was full, Jesus told his disciples, "Now gather the leftovers, so that nothing is wasted." So they picked up the pieces and filled twelve baskets with scraps left by the people who had eaten from the five barley loaves." (John 6:1-13 NLT)*

I heard God say that if we would only trust in Him and go ahead with the programme, He would finance His own project.

I gathered all my leaders and encouraged them with what The Lord had told me. That year, we went ahead with the conference. People gave willingly to finance the programme and in the end we were at a surplus. All glory to God!

4. The Word of Knowledge, Word of Wisdom and the Discerning of Spirits:

The Bible refers to three Gifts of the Holy Spirit: the word of knowledge, the word of wisdom and the discerning of spirits. These help the believer to know the mind of God and are usually referred to as revelatory gifts.

> *'For to one is given by the Spirit, the word of wisdom: to another the word of knowledge by the same Spirit' (1 Cor. 12:8 KJV)*

The gift of the word of knowledge is a supernatural revelation of God's mind about issues of the past and present. The word of wisdom relates to future events about people or things or events. These gifts from The Holy Spirit can enable you to know the mind of God about your spouse-to-be.

It is important for us to understand that these manifestations are in fact gifts; available to all believers who have the Holy Spirit. We should want and pray for them; though they are given as the Spirit wills. I must caution you however: If a believer, manifesting these gifts, speaks to you about your choice of a life partner, you should only take heed if it is confirmation of what God has spoken to you directly.

5. Dreams:

> *"And it shall come to pass afterward that I will pour out my spirit upon all flesh: and your sons and your daughters shall prophesy, your old men shall dream dreams, your young men shall see visions"* (Joel 2:28 KJV)

There are all kinds of dreams: many are not significant. Nonetheless, God leads through prophetic dreams. The right interpretation to the dream is important. In order to base your decisions on dreams, you need certainty that this is God's way of leading you. If it isn't, you cannot rely on them, and there is no need to insist on God using this channel. Key word: consistency.

A lady in my church once told me about how God had revealed her husband-to-be through a dream. A few years earlier, they had met at a friend's birthday party. Her friend had introduced her to him among other Christians and after the event, they went their separate ways. Days later, she had a dream and saw one of the guys from the party in a photograph hung in her living room; he was standing next her in a wedding dress. She did not share it with anyone because she did not know the young man. There had been no exchange of contacts. After a long time, a young man called her one day and expressed his interest in her. It was him! After this, they both sought God individually and got convinced about each other. Today they are happily married.

In The Bible, there are many examples of people who God led by dreams, both in The Old and The New Testament. The wise men were given a warning by God not to go back to King Herod to report where they had found Jesus. Joseph, the father of Jesus Christ, was also warned in a dream to take his family away to Egypt and when it was time to return from Egypt, he had a similar leading.

6. Visions:

'and it shall come to pass afterward, that I will pour out my spirit upon all flesh: and your sons and your daughters shall prophesy, your old men shall dream dreams, your young men shall see visions' (Joel 2:28 KJV).

Visions are different from dreams. Dreams are commonly during your sleep; while with visions, you are awake and your eyes are spiritually opened so you can see a picture or events. This gift is particularly manifested by mature Christians who spend good time alone with God. In order to depend on this gift, you need the proof of time. Key word: Consistency. The vision must agree with the Word of God. Again, we must not insist that God should lead us in any particular way; otherwise it will amount to laying fleeces before God. Laying a fleece implies dictating a particular method to God by which to lead you ; it is open to error.

7. Circumstance:

God can speak to a person using a particular circumstance. Usually this is more to confirm what he has spoken to you through other ways.

8. Another believer:

God can use another believer to confirm His will to you; your pastor, a prophet or any other believer. This however, is to confirm what God has already spoken to you in some way. You must not base your decision on the convictions of others only. Would your biological father choose a go-between to speak to you? Not unless you become rebellious and have lost your relationship with him. This is also true in our relationship with God. It is not scriptural for a 'New Testament Christian' to primarily rely only on being led by the prophet. Our God wants to keep up a father-son relationship with us. He wants to instruct, teach and guide you directly by His Spirit in you and by His Word.

> *'This is the third time I am coming to you. In the mouth of two or three witnesses shall every word be established.' (2 Corinthians 13:1 KJV)*

9. Intuition:

God speaks to a mind renewed by His Word. As The Word of God conditions the mind, it becomes aligned with The Holy Spirit. It becomes so sensitive that it mirrors The Mind of Christ. The conscience is troubled when one is out of tune with God's will.

The important fact to note about the various ways in which God leads His people, is that God speaks all the time. He is like a radio; we only pick His transmission when we tune in to the right frequency. So we all need to develop sensitivity to The Holy Spirit. This is part and parcel of growing as a Christian.

Every believer has at least one way in which The Lord speaks to them. It is their responsibility, however, to develop. Learn to stay quiet after prayer and expect the Lord to speak to you; do not rush out immediately.

We develop the habit of hearing from God when we lay a demand on Him to lead us in every little area of our lives. We may not get it right from the start, but with perseverance, we will grow and it eventually becomes our lifestyle.

Remember:

> *'As many as are led by the spirit of God are the sons and daughters of God'* (Romans 8:14)

You should not wait until the time you want to make big decision before you know how God speaks; it breeds uncertainty and confusion.

The message remains: Get intimate with God. Be serious in your walk with Him. The joy and greatest advantage of being a Christian is in the privilege of being led by God; our life decisions are not left to chance. There are no regrets in following God's will. What a great benefit that guarantees an inevitably fulfilling life!

CHAPTER SIX

Courtship from A Christian Perspective
SO HOLD MY HAND AND LET US RUN TOGETHER

Courtship from A Christian Perspective

> *"Fall in love with someone who deserves your heart, not someone who plays with it"*
> *(Author unknown)*

Courtship begins from the time two people agree to start a relationship till the day they get married. The main goal of courtship is to know, understand, adjust and build each other in preparation for marriage. In other words, courtship aims to secure the relationship.

As explained earlier, the aim of dating is simply getting to know another person as an acquaintance. The intention behind dating is for a guy to give a hint to the girl about his interest in her so that she can also pray about it. Courtship, however, involves a higher level of commitment. In this case, the two people would have already made up their minds to commit to a relationship with an intention to eventually culminate in marriage. We can compare it to the Jewish custom of betrothal or being espoused.

Courtship essentially involves getting to know and understand each other; going through a time of adjustment, learning to plan and work together, laying a good foundation for the future and getting to know the extended family.

Some essential ingredients required for a successful courtship include: reconciliation of values, adjusting to one another, sincere assessment of each other, praying and studying God's word together, effective conflict resolution, effective communication, transparency, keeping holy, willingness to learn and change, as well as undergoing marriage education. We will discuss these values in detail below.

- **RECONCILIATION OF VALUES**

To every Christian family, is a common culture; the culture of The Kingdom of God. The Bible presents to every family, or would-be family, Kingdom values and an orientation; in which both husband and wife should share and live by. The Bible gives a common philosophy for both spouses. This is the basis for the vows taken by both persons.

There are two main reasons that make the reconciling of values necessary:

Firstly, the two persons coming together into a lifelong relationship, having been brought up in two different homes, coming from different backgrounds and having had different experiences. The different backgrounds form the bases of their individual orientation in life; significantly influencing their views and lifestyles in different ways.

Secondly, these days, cross-cultural or cross-racial marriages are common occurrences and are on the increase. God is obviously not against this; when, if both parties involved are Christians with common beliefs and philosophies of life.

In my opinion, there exist three types of cultures:

a. *Kingdom culture*

This is a culture that is in keeping with or in line with Biblical precepts. However, different communities or races express it in peculiar ways. The specific expressions can differ in ways that obviously cannot all be stipulated in The Bible. For instance, there are different ways in which we show respect or honour parents and greet or interact with older people. Attitudes as well as the levels of relationships that exist towards the extended families and in-laws can differ in various cultures. Different cultures have diverse ways of expressing courtesy. Regardless of the differences of expression, however, The Bible has clear instructions for the Christian to live by these values. Your learning and understanding of such differences in the culture of your prospective spouse shall help you blend with the culture you shall eventually be a part of. This undoubtedly makes you more accepted, appreciated and loved; not only by your prospective spouse, but also members of their family.

b. Good practice

These are cultural practices that are not against Biblical principles, nor stipulated in The Bible. They are, in effect, good practice. These need discussion, understanding and upholding by both parties.

c. Cultures which are contrary to biblical principles

There are also cultures that are clearly against Biblical principles. These need discarding; no compromising. During courtship, any cultural practice classified under this category needs open discussion by the prospective spouses. They should use guidance from The Bible to agree on a common stand on such matters.

Indeed, there are several other factors that make it highly necessary to make effort in understanding and appreciating the cultural backgrounds of the person you intend to share the rest of your life with. The types of food you eat, the ways you care, how you relate with others, as well as many other things may differ. These differences will have implications, not only on your relationship with your spouse-to-be, but also your in-laws, spouse's friends and the new community you might end up relocating into after marriage.

The statement Ruth made in response to her mother-in-law holds a lesson for us:

> 'But Ruth replied, "Don't ask me to leave you and turn back. Wherever you go, I will go; wherever you live, I will live. Your people will be my people, and your God will be my God' (Ruth1:16 NLT)

- **ADJUSTING TO EACH OTHER**

"Adjustment is the act of bringing to proper relations / regulations / order" (Webster Dictionary)

Marriage is the closest relationship in life; more faithful than the relationship with children, parents, or s*iblings. It merges two independent people into "one flesh": 'Therefore shall a man leave his father and his mother, and shall cleave unto his wife: and they shall be one flesh. And they were both naked, the man and his wife, and were not ashamed'. (Gen 2:24-25 KJV).*

Marriage is like gluing two sheets of paper together. After the glue dries, it is impossible to separate them and have each sheet intact without deformity. This oneness initially takes place in the spirit: *'Didn't God make you one body and spirit with her? What was his purpose in this? It was that you should have children who are truly God's people. So make sure that none of you breaks his promise to his wife'* (Malachi 2:15). Marriage therefore changes both partners permanently.

The would-be couple need to understand however, that even though they become one by the marriage covenant, they are still different in the way they do and perceive things in practice; they are two people made one by God in Spirit. For the couple to take advantage of this spiritual transformation to bring lifelong happiness, they need to make some practical adjustments.

As explained earlier, this stems from the prospective couple having difference in family backgrounds, upbringing, interests, 'class', temperaments and so on. These differences, if not managed with the right attitude, could result in unhappiness. Positive adjustments in a marriage can transform both partners for the better. In other words, transformation depends on the couple's willingness to make some meaningful compromises; to avoid confusion and unnecessary misunderstanding, especially during the early years of the marriage. For this to happen, there are three things each prospective spouse must will to do:

1. *Compromise some values and practices that you have been accustomed to:*

Merging two people of different gender, backgrounds, training, upbringing, cultures, education, values, weaknesses, strengths, work schedules etc into a perfect 'one' is a daunting task; which should never be taken for granted! It is important to note that there are things we might be able to change in our partners, but there are also things that may never change. The success of the marriage, therefore, calls for the willingness to compromise some of our own values and things we cherish; for example hours of sleep, times to return home after work and many others.

2. *Change what needs to be changed in your spouse with patience and love*

Patience is a major key for success; even in those things that we consider necessary to change in our spouses. We should not expect habits or things developed over decades to vanish instantly. Always remember that true love will bring out the best in your spouse.

3. Adapt to what cannot be changed

You cannot change everything that you are unhappy about in your spouse, but you should have the willingness to adjust. Indeed, it will be wrong to go into a relationship with a mindset to change your spouse; you cannot change the core personality of a person. Insistence on changing every such thing in your spouse would only create tension and set the marriage on the rocks.

The following are some areas of concern that usually need some levels of adjustments in would-be couples.

- ### *Spiritual adjustments*

In some instances, a spouse is at a higher spiritual state than the other; for example with one feeling that the other is not very matured or not reading The Bible and praying as much. In such situations even spending time praying together could be a source of misunderstanding, with one feeling being slowed and the other feeling dragged. The best way out is not to keep at it as you used to in your own separate ways. The closer both of you are to God, the closer you are to each other. The spouse you fail to carry up the spiritual ladder is more likely to pull you down. If you usually shout at the top of your voice in prayer at dawn, do not consider your spouse demon possessed for suggesting that you reconsider the way, place and the times of the day you engage in such prayers.

- ### *Friendships and Relationships*

In a fulfilling marriage, a spouse is also a friend; the best friend. Other friends, no matter how relevant or close they were, should take second place in your relationships. With time, the couple must work towards maintaining common family friends who relate with both partners. Even if not towards that level of mutual friendship, it is useful to introduce your would-be-spouse to your friends. You may have to lose some friends, especially if your spouse indicates their displeasure or dislike of any.

- *Career / Job adjustments*

The success of a marriage may rest on the need to give up a well-paying job for a lower paying one or even become jobless for a while. One may need to re-locate. This should, however, be carefully discussed to meet the interests and ambitions of the family in question. This decision should be selfless and should also not be affected by your families and friends.

- *Passions, Interests and hobbies*

It is very helpful to set up some common grounds of passions, interests and hobbies. Developing interest in what your spouse is passionate about such as sports, games, issues on politics or even their career will invariably enrich your communication.

- *Your independence*

Marriage compromises one's independence; anyone who is not willing to do this cannot expect to have a happy marital life. You should not continue with the mentality that "this is my life and I choose to live it the way I want to". Once married, you can no longer choose to come home when you want; you may need to call home and seek your spouse's permission to keep staying out. These discussions are held during courtship.

There are several other areas where adjustment is necessary; depending on the uniqueness of the people involved in the relationship. These may include the following areas, which prospective couples could use as the focus of their discussions during their period of courtship:

- Background, orientation, family ties and belief systems.
- Ways of doing things; House management, organisation, orderliness, cleanliness, appetites.
- Anger management, rage, emotional display.
- Taboos.
- Likes and dislikes; holidays, menu, decorations.
- Personality differences and temperaments; one is an extrovert and the other an introvert or one is loud while the other may not be.
- Family demands and commitments; coping with jobs, children, the issue of having your first child.

The list can go on and on, but the important keys to effective adjustment include effective communication; learning to talk to each other. Talk, talk and talk. Be sure you are sincere and honest about your concerns. Say how you feel, but do so in love. Do not be offensive; it will result in self-defence by the other person. Also, listen and listen well to understand what the concerns of your spouse-to-be are.

Every person is unique in their wiring; we have different personalities. Though the level of one's Christian maturity may influence their personality, it will not change one's personality type altogether. It is important for those in the relationship to understand each other's types. We need to study the strengths and weaknesses of each other's unique personality types and be willing to discuss them openly; to make adjustments where necessary.

We all have our blind spots. These are areas of our lives that we cannot see by ourselves but others, especially our spouses, will see by reason of the close relationship; and point them out to us. We should readily own up to these shortcomings and be willing to deal with them. We must avoid being defensive, making excuses, or justifying any bad habits and attitudes. Rather, each person must readily learn from, and develop the positive areas in each other. Acknowledge and reinforce positive attitudes.

We must have a teachable and correctable Spirit. A teachable spirit is one of the character traits that you should look for in a potential mate. If a person is teachable, he or she will humbly listen to God, their pastor or mentor, and their future spouse when making decisions.

Each one of us should have an authority-figure over us. This could be your pastor and/or your mentor. It is good to also find out who plays that role of authority over the person you intend to marry. You must remember no one is perfect; not even you. So your partner, too, is not perfect.

If a man has glaring character defects, it is likely that he is not teachable: watch out!

Make adjustments; for both parties becoming a team with a common vision, mindset, lifestyle, attitude and view-point.

You should do all of these with The Word of God as the reference. Studying The Word of God together is a key reason in developing common orientation. Read relevant aspects of The Bible together and read other Christian books that deal with the areas in question. If there is any disagreement, it is always good to involve your mentor, pastor or a Christian counsellor. It is important to pray constantly for one another.

- **CONFLICT RESOLUTION**

In any relationship, there is conflict. I must quickly emphasise that it is not frequent; it is the exception and not the norm.

There are several reasons why conflicts arise in relationships. Among others, negative attitudes such as un-forgiveness, insecurity, pessimism, hatred, unhealthy jealousy, malice, stubbornness, nagging, not willing to listen and reason together to arrive at joint decisions, anger, selfishness and so on could be the cause of conflicts in relationships.

If there are conflicts most of the time you spend together or over every major issue, then there is something fundamentally wrong with the relationship. It might be worth having an honest look into both of you. This is a 'Red Flag'!

There are attitudes that are a bad omen for any relationship; these should never be ignored. The following are examples that you should deal with properly before going into marriage:

- Do you always claim you are Miss or Mr Right?
- Do any of you struggle to admit your faults when you are wrong?
- Do you argue a lot?
- Do you keep malice for days?
- Do you struggle to forgive when you hurt each other?
- Do you readily make references to past settled issues when there are disagreements?
- Do you make references to completely unrelated faults of the other as weapons to prove their own actions; when correcting them?
- Do you find it difficult to say 'I am sorry' or apologise?

- Do you compare your partner to someone else?
- Do you have a history of losing many friends in the past?
- Are you violent, verbally abusive, aggressive, or do you have an explosive character?
- Have you ever, hit, pushed or even pointed fingers in misconduct when angry?
- Anytime there is a conflict, do you readily involve your friends or your parents?

A yes answer to any of the above questions is a good ground for discussion. The fewer yeses the better. Never ignore these issues; you must work together to encourage changes in any area of need. You may read books that deal with such character flaws.

The two people in the relationship must learn to resolve their issues of conflict completely, as soon as possible. It is best to learn to settle your own issues without involving a third person. In case of a major issue, it will be necessary to involve your mentor, counsellor or pastor; but do not make it routine. It is strongly advisable not to involve your parents in any conflict involving both of you.

> *"And 'don't sin by letting anger control you.' Don't let the sun go down while you are still angry, for anger gives a foothold to the devil".* (Ephesians 4:26, 27 NLT)

- **COMMUNICATION: PURSUING DEEPER KNOWLEDGE OF EACH OTHER**

Communication could be verbal and non verbal. When courting, you aim to become the best of friends. In verbal communication, you must work hard to make yourself understood and understand your partner. You must understudy each other's body language and learn to respond to them appropriately. It is important that you closely observe one another as this is the time in which you learn to actively listen and work together; to lay a strong foundation for your marriage.

This is a time to read books together and learn more about each other. It is also a time to engage in active discussions about everything and arrive at conclusions together. You have to learn to communicate your feelings effectively to each other. Be on the lookout for things like personality profile, family background, life history, leadership ability, sense of humour, future ambitions, social tastes, friends, use of tongues, the reaction to good and bad news and general comportment during unguarded moments such as at play. Also, watch each other's attitude to money and properties, respect, discipline, instructions, obedience, correction and disagreements.

This period is a time of discovery and knowing each other. It is the time to find out each other's strengths, weaknesses and differences with a desire to know where to help each other improve. As much as possible, take note of the information you receive from friends, parents, other believers and pastors.

Very importantly, you need to share your past experiences with each other including past mistakes, failures and successes. It is a time to discuss everything necessary and important for both of you and the relationship; do not hide anything! You should not hide anything from your partner which could cause embarrassment or problems for the marriage in future if discovered. Openness, sincerity, integrity and trust are very important virtues. They are the true tests of a person's character, they are fundamental to relationship building and oneness.

'And they were both naked, the man and his wife, and were not ashamed' (Genesis 2: 25)

The truth is if you cannot accept your partner just as they are, having known the truth about him or her, you may need to ask yourself again if you truly love this person and if you were really convinced about being together. This is the test of true acceptance. It will help bring the two of you to a point of full commitment and help you not to go back on the relationship. It is necessary to totally open up to your partner during this phase of the relationship.

Among other things, you need to discuss financial matters during this period. For example, 'How can we be one in our finances?' Should we keep a joint account or personal account? The focus of your conversations may include the type of wedding you want, where to live after the wedding, which Church to attend especially if you are not attending the same church, issues about work, size of family and many more. These are important areas of discussion in which you may need to agree before the wedding.

> *'Can two walk together except they be agreed?'* (Amos 3:3KJV)

- **BE TRANSPARENT**

Transparency breeds trust. To make sure of this, you will need to disclose the major mistakes of your past, relationships, health issues, weaknesses and the like. A relationship without trust is unhealthy. Do not be disguised, pretend or lie to each other; any of these will breed mistrust. You must talk about everything; including issues about your families.

> *'And they were both naked, the man and his wife, and were not ashamed'* (Genesis 2: 25)

- **COMMUNION WITH GOD**

A very important experience during courtship is when both of you spend meaningful and quality time to pray, fast and study The Bible together. This helps to build you up as people and helps you build each other up. During such moments, you commit yourselves, your plans and any envisaged challenges to God. It is also a time to pray for your future home, where you will settle as a family, the children you want from God and even the provisions for your marriage. Communion with God is a good habit that you cultivate during courtship; it will eventually become part of your marital life. Remember that:

> *Without the help of the Lord it is useless to build a home or to guard a city Psalm 127:1(CEV).*

- **MENTORING**

Chose a mentor in courtship; one whom both parties agree on. A family you both appreciate and admire; a family who epitomises your dream home. Also, you should both respect the family and be happy to submit to them; one who can correct and instruct you or whose view you will accept for when both of you disagree during courtship. Having a mentor is essential because you will have questions you both cannot answer. In courtship, there will be areas of disagreement; you will have various issues to resolve and need a practical guide.

- **MARRIAGE EDUCATION/MARRIAGE LESSONS**

This is a necessity for two people going into a marriage relationship. Just like driving, no one begins to drive a vehicle just because they have been in the passenger seat watching someone else drive for years. The assumption that because a person has, 'grown up in a good family', he or she will be a good husband or wife, is not always true. This is not automatic. One may come from a good home where daddy and mummy have been role models; this however, does not automatically equip the person adequately for marriage. It is true however, that coming from a good family setting will certainly put one at an advantage; it does not automatically guarantee that you're able to effectively function as a husband or a wife.

The reason is that your spouse is different from your father or mother. Consequently, the dynamics in your own home will be uniquely different. There is, therefore, the need to undergo pre-marriage counselling or marriage education. This could be with your pastor. You may also take advantage of marriage seminars and workshops to equip yourselves for this all important journey of marriage. All of these will prepare you and equip you for your responsibilities as a husband or wife; and later as a father or mother. It will also help you to better handle other factors that may affect your family. It will give you the solid foundation you need.

- **MARRIAGE PREPARATION SHOULD BEGIN NOW**

It is good to prayerfully consider your wedding date as early as possible in your courtship. This is for your planning. This date need not be publicised yet; your parents or friends do not have to know. It allows you to have a timeline to work towards; even if all you can decide on is a particular year. Later, as you plan with the family and your church, you will then be able to arrive at a precise month and day.

- **KEEP YOURSELF HOLY**

To keep God in your relationship, be pure. Courtship or engagement is not equal to marriage. If you want to please God, conduct your relationship with the reverential fear of God. Sex is not for dating or the courting period. Reserve it for marriage. You must decide early in your courtship that you will not have pre-marital sex; go ahead and set the boundaries and keep to them. Manage this decision daily. Sexual sin is a cankerworm that destroys marriage foundations. You should avoid things that will weaken your resolve and make you vulnerable.

> *'Run from anything that stimulates youthful lusts. Instead, pursue righteous living, faithfulness, love, and peace. Enjoy the companionship of those who call on the Lord with pure hearts.' (2 Timothy 2:22 NLT)*

Avoid being alone together in secret places, staying up late together at night and sleeping in the same room or alone in the same house. Avoid kissing, petting, caressing and so on; these normally lead to sexual sin. Do not be so confident; anyone can fall into sexual sin if care is not taken. Do not play with fire, it burns!

- ***Problems resulting from pre-marital sex***

Premarital sex poses many problems; they include the following:

1. It is a sin that will haunt you throughout life; do everything in your power to avoid it.
2. It leads to lack of trust in each other after you've been married.
3. Statistics show that it contributes to higher rate of divorce.
4. It is exposes one to sexually transmitted diseases.
5. It could also lead to unplanned pregnancy.

- **HOW LONG SHOULD COURTSHIP LAST?**

There is no hard and fast rule about the length of courtship. This depends on how effective the courtship has been. For instance, have you understood each other well enough? Have you attained a state of true harmony and unity? It involves understanding your partner's mindset, thought pattern, points of view, philosophy of life, attitudes, plans, dreams and aspirations.

Moreover, you need to understand and agree to each other's stand on important issues. You should also consider your readiness for marriage in terms of basic needs like accommodation, jobs, financial status, and so on. Your ability to keep up purity is equally important, as you may need to shorten the length of courtship if you honestly know it will help prevent falling into sin. Finally, you both need to emotionally, physically and spiritually be ready for marriage.

All in all, you should not go into marriage if there are still unresolved issues or differences. Both of you should arrive at a point where you know and both agree that you are ready for the marital journey ahead. At this point, you should begin to take necessary the steps towards preparation for the wedding.

Chapter Seven

Watch Out for Red Flags In a Relationship

Watch Out For Red Flags In A Relationship

Being in a relationship is so exciting that you can easily be carried away by the euphoria of it; failing to see the warning signs even when they are clear. Have you been dating or courting someone for some time? Have you identified any strengths and weaknesses? This is normal.

No two people are exactly the same; everyone is unique. However, as explained earlier, there is the need for mutual adjustments, and you should both be willing to do so. It is possible for you to have discovered some character flaws that have left you wondering whether you should go ahead! Do not ignore them, but rather, deal with them in accordance to the standards of God's Word.

The goal of courtship is marriage. However, there could be ground for the courtship not to go ahead into a marriage relationship. This chapter aims to discuss this. There are many factors which tend to make it difficult to break up a courtship; even when there are obvious warning signs or major differences that could not be resolved.

Such factors include the following:

The length of time the two people have been in the relationship. The longer the period, the more difficult it is to consider breaking away from it; even when there are clear signals that things won't work. Also, the thought that one is getting old, especially for a lady, makes turning away from a relationship harder.

On some occasions, the notion that family members and friends, who have known about the relationship, will find a break up very disappointing, is the reason. This is particularly the case if the family members happen to like the spouse-to-be. My close relative gave this same reason for continuing in a courtship that led to her troubled married life years later.

Other sentiments that people base their decision on ignoring obvious red flags in their courtship include: Friends passing comments such as; 'You two are such a perfect match, you are so lucky to have each other!', 'You're so beautiful and he's so handsome; what a beautiful couple!'.

The guy or girl may also be thinking; 'Oh that person has a good sense of humour, they have a good job, their parents really like me and have even given me gifts, our family and friends are already asking us for our wedding plans!'. The possible thoughts are endless. Some may wonder, 'Where would I start if I end this relationship?' or, 'After all these years? Let me just keep going on and sweat it out'. Furthermore, when people are desperate for marriage, they are likely to turn blind eyes and ears to visible and audible red flags; more so when other friends are in stable relationships or are getting married.

Unfortunately, none of these factors is strong enough to make your marriage succeed when there are major issues that cannot be resolved. Be true and sincere to yourself; whatever you get or keep by compromise, you will either regret or lose altogether.

Remember, marriage is a lifelong relationship. Also bear in mind that God hates divorce. Besides, many say that the emotional pain of divorce is so devastating that it is only second in intensity to the death of a loved one. Divorce has trans-generational implications on children, grand children, great grand children and generations to come.

Therefore, when you find red flags in your relationship, it is only wise that you pause to think and sincerely ask yourself genuine questions. If necessary, involve your mentor or your pastor. It is in your best interest to make decisions and take actions that will prevent future heartache, sorrow and weeping.

Emotions can blindfold. Nonetheless, you will need to decide what you want to do with the relationship, all by yourself. No one else can do this for you. It is good if you take time to personally think about your relationship and consider the red flags. You must not go into any relationship or continue in it with the mindset to change the other person; this is often impossible. You can only change yourself. You don't stand to gain anything by walking into a lifetime of painful regret, especially when it could be avoided.

Marriage is a great gift from God. It is a great blessing and a source of unparalleled lifelong support; customised by God for every person. The period of courtship is the time to look carefully at your partner; it is the time you should sincerely study and check them. You should not postpone this until after the exchange of rings. God wants to lead and guide you in the way you will go. He wants you to involve Him in your courtship and marriage. He ultimately knows the end from the beginning.

It is therefore necessary to have a sense of the Holy Spirit as He leads us; we should not rely only on our own understanding. We should also not turn deaf ears to the advice of the godly people who God has placed in our lives.

> *'Trust in the Lord with all thine heart; and lean not unto thine own understanding. In all thy ways acknowledge him, and he shall direct thy paths. Be not wise in thine own eyes: fear the Lord, and depart from evil'* (Proverbs 3:5-7 KJV).

You may say love is blind, but I say marriage is an eye opener. I have had opportunities to ask friends, whose relationship was turbulent or ended in divorce, questions about what went wrong. Most of the time, they lamented and admitted that either God warned them or that they saw enough red flags, which they ignored; hoping that things would change!

Some people prove themselves by saying things like, 'No one is perfect, all guys are the same; there are no Angels, what is important is being the right person and not necessarily finding the right person.' And so on. We, however, need to apply wisdom; be sensible and not foolish. The truth is it does matter who you marry. This is the reason it is important that you involve God in your decision-making right from the start. Again, this is in our long-term best interest. God is our Shepherd and He loves and cares about you and I; we are special to Him.

No matter how excited you are in a relationship, it is important that you consider red flags; and do not ignore or excuse them. Sometimes, Christian friends or the people well acquainted with the person you are going out with; having observed their attitude in different settings; try to draw your attention to the truth about your partner's spiritual state or a hidden character. Unfortunately, sometimes, your response is so abrupt that the person may even regret pointing it out to you. Sometimes, you swing into defence of your partner using statements like; 'He believes in God, she's quite busy with work that's why you don't see her in church, he comes to church with me and I believe he will come to faith after we marry, he doesn't stop me from going to church, she loves me, he is nice; in fact his behaviour is better than the 'so-called' Christians, she is very caring and considerate' and many more.

Again, be sincere with yourself. No one has the power to change or convert another person. So do not indulge in self-delusion; it is dangerous. It is God in us and a fear for Him that makes a life good.

> 'Do not be unequally yoked together with unbelievers . . .
> '(2 Corinthians 6:14)

Historically, 'yoke' is an agricultural term. A yoke is placed on the necks of two oxen, to enable them to effectively pull an agricultural tool;

making ridges or harvesting crops. For the two yoked animals to work effectively and share the burden equally, making 'life' easier for both, they must walk in the same direction and at a similar pace. This is the principle underpinning yoking. In a situation where these conditions are not in place, the result is that the two animals work in different directions. Under such conditions, they will inflict pain on each other; wearing each other out as well as being unproductive. God does not want two people who are planning a lifelong covenant marriage together, to have unequal or different philosophies of life. It will result in pain, frustration, struggle and disagreement. It does not work!

Let us look at some examples of Red flags:

There are emotional red flags such as anger, lack of self-control, selfishness and hypersensitivity. Anger is a God-given emotion. People may have legitimate reasons for getting angry, but there are also opportunities to deal with it appropriately. Control your anger; do not allow it to take control of your actions.

> 'And "Don't sin by letting anger control you." Don't let the sun go down while you are still angry, for anger gives a foothold to the devil.' (Ephesians 4:26, 27 NLT)

If your partner beats you up in your relationship, it will inevitably increase to a higher level after marriage.

> 'Do not make friends with a hot-tempered man; do not associate with one easily angered'. (Proverb 22:24 NIV)

The point being made here is that a man, who in courtship, beats or throws objects at you; destroying any item in the house when angry, should not even be trusted with your life and future. This is an example of a red flag that you must not ignore. There is no place for violent behaviour, physical, emotional or verbal abuse in a relationship. It is a major red alert that you must deal with.

Lack of self-control is another key issue to look into: Does your spouse-to-be follow through on commitments and plans? Are they able to hold a job? Are they in debt because of impulse spending? Can they control their passions?

Selfishness is another major red flag: Do they always seek to have their way? Is it just about him or her? Do their lives revolve around themselves? You should sort out all selfishness before marriage as it will continue if you do nothing. Another thing is to watch their action towards others in need.

> 'Each of you should look not only to your own interests, but also to the interest of others.' (Philippians 2:4 NIV)

You need assurance that your wife or husband to-be does not have a victim perspective or mentality. Do they take responsibility for their struggles or simply blame it on others? It is necessary for us to get past our pain so we can move forward. Can they own up to their short comings? It is possible to put up with this for a while when the romantic feelings are sky-high, but what happens when those feelings calm down and you settle into reality? It is not easy to make any change after marriage.

Character red flags are also very crucial: Some of these are actions that cause you to control other such as, dictatorship, domination and manipulation. Others are actions that control you such as dishonesty, addictions, the inability to apologise and the unwillingness to get help. If you see glimpses of these now, it is likely to increase in marriage.

It is not God's intention to have the husband, the head, as over-controlling. Jesus is our model of headship. He led by loving to the point of laying his life down for us. Marrying a controlling husband will, undoubtedly, affect the harmony in the home.

On the other hand, a woman who has experienced control or abuse while growing up may find it difficult to submit to a husband; as directed in The Scriptures. A woman with this background, though married to a loving husband, is likely to entertain the fear that her submission may give room to his domination. It is important, therefore, to deal with such past experiences; doing away with them for the sake of having a lovely future.

Dishonesty can easily be overlooked in a relationship. Trust is the backbone of a relationship. Once trust is gone, there is no relationship as such; it bases on assumption and accusation, and not on sincere communication.

> 'Truthful lips endure forever, but a lying tongue lasts only a moment.'(Proverbs 12:19 NIV)

As mentioned earlier, your spouse-to-be is more like your best friend. Lying may have a momentary purpose but, it will eventually lead to destruction. Can you trust your 'best friend'? Is the truth being compromised for gain in your relationship?

Addictions, in the form of substance abuse, eating disorders, or those of a sexual nature, will destroy a marriage. Seek for help; address addiction, do not overlook it.

Does your 'best friend' accept it when they are wrong? Do they acknowledge their errors or mistakes? To set up a healthy marriage, you must deal with this. How do they react to correction? How willing are they to seek for help?

It is also important to consider issues like dependency: Being over dependant has the tendency of suffocating the other person. Similarly, an independent attitude, where the person is rigid and inflexible, is dangerous.

It must also be borne in mind to keep the relationship non-exclusive; any relationship that takes you away from your family and/or friends, calls for careful reconsideration. You need freedom to relate or interact with other people. There is the need to acknowledge the changes to put into effect using The Word of God as standard, before you go into marriage. If in doubt, seek counsel from your pastor, your mentor or a Christian marriage counsellor.

It is necessary to keep an open mind and eyes to all these warning signs; dealing with them as much as possible in courtship. Seek God's counsel, prayerfully and sincerely. Do not forget that you and your spouse must have at least one authority figure over your lives; a person that you submit to. However, it is advisable that once you are courting, both of you should have the same authority figure over you. A person with no authority figure, or who does not submit to anyone, is a clear red flag. Such people are not accountable. They are uncontrollable and you will find it difficult to correct them when things go wrong.

A broken courtship is better than a broken marriage. Remember: Do not go ahead into marriage if you have not resolved The Red flags!

CHAPTER EIGHT

Preparing for your Wedding
...IT'S MY DAY!

Preparing for your Wedding

To fail to plan is to plan to fail!

This is your wedding; it is a one-time event. It is important that both of you take responsibility for what you want and who you want there. You must constantly check the progress; through effective and consistent communication between you and your spouse-to-be. This is a good opportunity for you and your spouse to gauge your communication skills and your ability to plan and organise together.

I must emphasise that you should avail yourself the opportunity for advice all the way through; especially from one or two of your friends who were successful in the planning of their marriages. Your pastors, counsellors, friends and parents are also there to make recommendations; be open to words of counsel.

In this section, I will attempt to briefly discuss some important issues to consider during the planning stage; these, however, are by no means exhaustive.

Spiritual Preparation

There are three significant times in life in which you are the main focus of the day. The day you are born, the day you get married and the day of your funeral.

Of these three, the only one which involves you in executing is your marriage. The wedding day is such an important occasion in your life and the spiritual events of the day can decide the eventual failure or success of the marriage relationship afterwards. You must therefore prepare spiritually. Spiritual preparation must involve prayer. It is in prayer you hand over the event and the people who are involved into God's hands.

'Commit thy way unto the LORD; trust also in him; and he shall bring it to pass.' (Psalm 37:5 KJV)

The devil attacked the first marriage in the Garden of Eden. He still attacks marriages, not only when they are well established, but also during preparation and in the laying of the foundation. Prevention is better than cure; resist the devil and his agents. Exercise spiritual authority over everything; praying for:

- Yourselves: For strength, wisdom, patience, guidance, protection, provision, good health and favour, as well as your families.
- All the people involved: The ministers, people you will delegate duties to, your venues, the organisation and the atmosphere.
- Your marriage: The wedding is only a day's event, but marriage is for life. Your prayer may involve regular fasting according; to the grace you have.

The spiritual preparation also involves studying the word of God together; to build your faith in God and take hold of His promises for yourselves and the marriage. God rewards your Faith in Him; you must not allow fear to have the upper hand over you. God is faithful. He is the 'More-than-enough God'; the 'El Shaddai'.

Spiritual preparation is easier when partners do not have anything to hide from each other. As discussed in the chapter on courtship, it is good for your spouse-to-be to know your past no matter how bad it is; this will prevent any surprises in the run up to the wedding or after.

You may come under a lot of pressure; preparing for this kind of ceremony has a way of getting on your nerves. Your patience is under trial at this time, so, pray for patience throughout. You must stay calm, without fret or worry; have confidence in God.

Choosing your wedding day
This is your day; however you must involve God by seeking His help. In arriving at the date, the parents of both the Bride and Groom and the priest of the Church in which the wedding will take place must agree. They all need carrying along as part of the decision-making. Bear in mind that this date is subject to availability of the Ministers who will officiate, the church and the reception venue. It is important that you give long enough notices.

Marriage education and counselling, or attending marriage seminars, are an essential part of your preparation for the wedding day and the marriage itself. Counselling is a pre-condition in most churches before being joined together in marriage. You must give enough notice to the church so that you can go through the entire process of counselling.

Besides being a prerequisite to being joined together in the church, it offers you a solid foundation for your marital life. Every church has its own program and protocol that they follow; you need to find out what this is well ahead of time. The marriage counsellors will also help you to get wisdom nuggets for your wedding day. You must ask questions.

What You Need
You must have a list of what you need for your wedding. This is usually a growing list; as you remember, you add to it. As you meet each need, you should tick it off. What you need determines who you need.

Who You Need
You should devise a list of who you need. This will contain the people who will undertake certain duties for you. They include: your bridal train, your event planners in some cases, the decorator, the caterer, the printer and so on. It is usually good to have a planner for this

event. This takes the stress off you and your spouse-to-be. If your budget cannot afford a professional event planner, you can always ask a friend or a close relative to take up that role.

Again, the list is endless; you continue to add to it as you check your progress. It is important to supervise and watch whatever you delegate. You must not make assumptions or take anything for granted. Regular meetings with your delegates, collectively or individually, are important.

You also need to have your to-do list. This is best done daily and weekly to help check progress.

Budgeting
The budget is dependent on your needs. Likewise, your needs depend on your budget. Arrange your budget in order of priority and constantly check it.

Your friends and family members may want to support you; having a budget helps them know how to do so. Be careful not to overspend. Avoid being in debt after your wedding as much as possible; this creates a major strain on you and your spouse.

Time Keeping
Being disciplined with time-keeping is one factor that you should not ignore. Punctuality encompasses integrity, competence and how much you value people; including yourself. Bear this in mind up until your wedding day.

Concluding remarks:
It is vital that you uphold God's standard throughout each process. From the processes of Dating and Courtship to Marriage; and all the stages they each entail. Above all, aim to glorify God.

I admonish you to decide to build your home and your future in the Lord, the Rock of ages, and on the principles of His word. As you do, you will enjoy His presence. This will, without doubt, make your home stand strong, united, fruitful, peaceful and triumphant. With that in place, no matter the general circumstances; you will ultimately succeed. Our Lord Jesus says;

> *"These words I speak to you are not incidental additions to your life, homeowner improvements to your standard of living. They are foundational words, words to build a life on. If you work these words into your life, you are like a smart carpenter who built his house on solid rock. Rain poured down, the river flooded, a tornado hit—but nothing moved that house. It was fixed to the rock. "But if you just use my words in Bible studies and don't work them into your life, you are like a stupid carpenter who built his house on the sandy beach. When a storm rolled in and the waves came up, it collapsed like a house of cards." (Matthew 7:24-27 MSG)*

It is my prayer and wish for you to have a strong foundation for your home and an exemplary future full of God's rich blessings.

May God bless you!